xvi
xiv
xxi

p 31 Shadowlands
p 40 'not to be interested in you'

SPARKS

SPARKS

JAMES LOW

Published by Simply Being www.simplybeing.co.uk

British Library Cataloguing in Publication Data. A catalogue record for this book is available from the British Library.

ISBN: 978-0-9569239-4-3

The image of Samantabhadra on page xiv was taken with thanks from the website of "The Great Middle Way". *https://greatmiddleway.wordpress. com/2011/04/25/king-of-aspiration-prayers/*

The image of Machig Labdron on page xiv was taken from the blog "Buddhist quote of the day" *https://garywonghc.wordpress.com/2014/11/*

The photo of CR Lama on page x appears on the website of Dzogchen Urgyen Ling. *http://dzogchenurgyenling.dk/english/teachers/chhimed-rigdz-in-rinpoche/*

The image on the front cover and the image on the back cover were both taken from *www.pexels.com.*

The image of Padmasambhava on page vi is taken with thanks from artwork of Katharina Winkelmann.

With thanks to everyone whom we have been able to identify and credit. Thanks also to those whom we have not been able to identify and credit.

Printed and bound in Great Britain by Lightning Source

DEDICATED
TO
THE POOR IN HEART

This busy world and our busy mind
Combine to keep us spinning
Remembering you breaks the spell
And brings a new beginning

Contents

Bright sun, shooting star
Lightning flash, buddha spark
Smiling bringer of peace
Melting the hardest heart

Preface

This is a book of gestures, of patterns expressing the connectivity which is the ground and source of our brief lives as sentient beings, beings who sense and feel and think and communicate.

The ground of our being is openness, unfettered awareness present in every event. We emerge within this field of light and illuminate and reflect each other. Sparks fly when we are touched and moved and perhaps such sparks can touch and move others. One spark from the bright fire of emptiness can start a conflagration burning all constructs to ashes. This loss is the true gain, the revelation of illusion.

Sparks emanate from the fire. They are the gift of the fire and show the way back to the fire. The fire of awareness burns bright in all of us, yet is usually taken for granted. Engaging with the sparks in this book invites us to be the open awareness which is the ground or basis of the reader, the thinker, the experiencer. This awareness, our awareness, is the spacious illuminating fire which sets alight all the varied moments of our lives.

These brief expressions arose within my experience of dharma. They were spoken and written over twenty or so years and reflect the moods of many different occasions. I hope they speak to you. The style is not formal and hopefully this loose texture makes the content easy to access and reflect on. Although some of the extracts have been organised around certain themes there is no progressive sequence in their ordering. You can start at any point and each spark or snippet is complete in itself. Reading is a whole-person activity – we receive most if we engage with our life experience and our clarity and allow our emotions and sensations to become part of the evolving picture.

Many of the pieces offered here are extracts from transcripts of talks I have given in Dharma centres in Europe. They were extracted by transcribers, primarily by Sarah Allen and Jo Féat, and by Barbara Terris.

Forming a book from fragments takes time, thoughtfulness and many drafts. The patient and thoughtful help of Barbara Terris has made this process possible. The book was set up for printing by Sarah Allen.

> Life is simple
> when you accept that it is complicated.
> Life is complicated
> when you believe it should be simple.

Dark buddha, first breath before dawn,
Silent still source of mind's effulgence
Open, available, our unchanging ground
Unobscured by deluded self-indulgence.

Spacious hospitality free of bias
Welcoming the fragments of disintegration
Like snowflakes falling on a lake
Dissolving in effortless self-liberation.

Introduction

Let's start at the very beginning; it's a very good place to start. What is life? Where do I come from? Who am I? When we pose these questions we look for answers – and so many answers are available. We can read of the origins of everything and learn that there was a Big Bang. We can learn about the formation of planet earth and the first signs of life and the many stages of evolution from that first dynamic formation. We can learn about the history of our country, our culture, our family, our parents' relationship and the factors which led to our conception. All this information comes to us in the form of stories. We hear the stories and form our sense of the world and our place in it out of these stories. We are part of the ongoing conversation within which we hear stories, formulate our response, and then speak our contribution. We are both shaped by and shaping of the narratives in which we move and live. We tell ourselves versions of what we have been told and in this way we become part of our culture.

When we ask, "Who am I?" we continue our habit of reliance on narrative. "Who am I? Well, let me tell you…" and off we go telling our stories of events, desires, interests, fears, hopes, traumas. There seems to be no end to the stories we can tell about ourselves as we move seamlessly from one topic to another, weaving a texture of recollection and emotion that seems both real and true. We seem to be talking about ourselves, describing ourselves, but perhaps we are, again and again, talking ourselves into existence. In each new situation of communication we form particular patterns of self-presentation that will allow us to see ourselves and to be seen by others as worthy of attention and of validation as being who we say we are. If this is so then we are the children of Scheherazade, maintaining our life by the flow of our beguiling stories.

The content of the story, what we say, is our primary focus. But who is the speaker, the storyteller? *"That's easy, I am the one who is telling the story.*

I am me! Let me tell you about me..." and off we go again creating castles in the air with our fascinating concepts. Round and round, on and on, from birth to death we swim in an ocean of concept, narrative, history, memory – accounts of events, facts, people, places. Usually we believe that this is simply how life is, this is what it means to be a human being, a member of the most intelligent and creative species on the planet.

But perhaps this reality we believe in is not quite what it seems. Perhaps the answers come and go so thick and fast we are blinded by the shining snowflakes of these representations which affirm the validity of self and other. Who am I? I am here, now, breathing in and out, alive – who is doing this, who is this happening to and for? If we just pause and allow space before we tell ourselves a selection from our vast repertoire of answers then there is the space in which we are revealed to ourselves. This offers us a glimpse of the face we had before we were born into the matrix of concepts. This is the ground of our being, the basis for all that we experience, including ourselves.

The desire to see with fresh eyes, to see without the opacity of assumption and projection, is the foundation of Buddhism. Two thousand five hundred years ago the pampered and protected young Siddhartha, the one who would become the Buddha, ventured out of the pleasure gardens within which he had been raised. He encountered sights that did not fit with what he had been told. He saw a sick person, an old person, a corpse and a wandering seeker after truth. These sights disrupted the totalising stories he had grown up with and he saw that there was more to life than he thought.

By putting into question the ready-made answers and beliefs that had sustained him, Siddhartha felt the fresh wind of freedom. He left home in search of the meaning of life and the origin of suffering. He went on a journey and in so doing he took his place in the long line of travellers on the Hero's Journey. He travelled here and there, finding new ideas, new forms of yoga and austerity, on and on, more and more, until eventually he got tired, *"Is there no end to this?"* Looking for an end to the endless road only serves to extend our journey beyond the horizon.

So he sat under a bodhi tree and did nothing. A lot happened to him – exciting visions, frightening visions, all kinds of moods and feelings, all the familiar constituents of his sense of self. But he just sat. The experiences came and went and he was still there, not as the narrative construct he had taken himself to be but as the open awareness that illuminates everything without itself being something that can be grasped. He was settled in the ground of experience as the illuminator of experience which is not itself an experience. This is beyond concepts – it can be lived but not said.

This is the foundation of all the schools and methods of Buddhism. Buddhism is not a path of dogma for there is no suggestion that beliefs about something are sufficient for awakening. Adopting a new identity and becoming a Buddhist is not the same as being buddha, awake, present.

Whether the thoughts we rely on are selfish or altruistic, worldly or spiritual, they can operate as a veil to the openness of being. When our thoughts are the limit of our experience, we revolve within the seeming facticity of what we encounter, making choices on the basis of our sense of who we are. "*I know what I like and I like what I know.*" In this way our potential is limited as both object, what we encounter, and subject, the one who encounters, are defined and developed within our habitual narrative: we think and talk ourselves and our world into existence.

This immersion in our thoughts, feelings, memories and so on as the means of generating meaning and value has us travelling on and on, with each seemingly final destination being revealed on arrival as just a different form of movement.

The ego is born from the illusion of separation, the sense of self being split off from environment. Our ego then maintains itself through identifying options and making choices on the basis of either/or, rather than both/and. It shapes itself through deciding what is right or best, and what it wants and what it tries to avoid. This choosing is intolerant of the whole, of everything. Choices are made in terms of our specific interests, of our concerns. They are grounded in partiality, in finding some particular aspects of the field to be better than others – not just more useful, but better. Seeing some aspects of the environment as intrinsically better than others confirms the hierarchy of values, and finding our niche in this helps us maintain our sense of self, the continuity of our personal identity. The desire to find better options keeps the self-referential ego orientated towards the future, towards progression to somewhere better.

The path to awakening is not a path from here to there. It is the path of the non-path from the idea of here to the non-conceptual actuality of here. The actuality of here is primary, intrinsic. It is not a concept, an idea, an account, an interpretation. But neither does it block ideas and interpretations for they are part of the flow of the pattern-making creativity of awareness, the clarity that is always already here and now without being discoverable anywhere as something fixed and enduring.

Within the vast family of buddhism the approach of dzogchen is particularly helpful for focusing on the key issues of who we are. Dzogchen means the great completion. 'Completion' indicates that there is nothing to be done, no improvement or development is required. 'Great' indicates emptiness, the absence of inherent self-nature, the absence of all definable and defining essence and substance. Dzogchen is who we are. Each living being, each individual, is part of the whole and partakes of that wholeness. We suffer and wander in confusion when we do not rest in and as that whole, when we take 'individual' to refer to the separate entity that I take myself to be, the one who stands apart. Awakening to the actuality of wholeness is liberation from the delusion of separation.

If it is this simple, if I am already basically okay, if I am part of the whole, why don't I know this? The whole is not a thing. It is not an object of knowledge. Learning some ideas about 'it' is not the same as finding oneself at home in 'it'. It is not something you can get a handle on – it has no handles, no edges, no cracks. You, the person looking, cannot find it if you continue to look in your habitual way. We need to relax and receive what we see without interfering with what is. The ego seeks identity through opinions and actions which alter what arises. When we open to what is, there is simple clarity illuminating both object and subject. With this immersion in radiance we are the unchanging truth of what and how we have always been and what and how the world has always been.

We need to make contact with the lineage of awakening. Although from the very beginning we have been part of the whole we cannot see this without the help of another. This fact may feel like a terrible insult to our ego. After all, we are educated, we are competent, we can make sense of what is going on. This is all true. We can make sense of what is going on because we are part of what is going on – and what is going on is all we know. This is our limit, our accumulation, our totality. We take a part, our part, to be the whole and it is this which keeps us functionally apart from the whole, the infinite whole from which we have never actually been parted.

The dzogchen lineage begins with wholeness shining forth as the primordial Buddha, Kuntu Zangpo. His name means 'always already good, perfect, complete' for he is the shining presence of wholeness. His fullness enlivens Dorje Sempa, 'indestructible being', who shows the purity of the mind untouched by obscuration. In turn Dorje Sempa's simplicity enlivens Garab Dorje, 'indestructible satisfaction', the satisfaction of completion. Garab Dorje manifested in our world and this was the beginning of the lineage of awakening to wholeness which has come down unbroken through time and is now available to us as the dzogchen teachings.

Garab Dorje set out all that was required in three brief statements: be invited to open to intrinsic presence, the basis your existence; do not remain in doubt about this; continue contentedly in this without seeking anything else.

The first point is direct introduction. This has two aspects which have to be synchronised so that the synergy of their non-duality opens the space of revelation. Direct introduction means finding the beginning, the ground, the base, the source, the starting point. It is there, in fact it is here, now, for it is the ground of our being, our existence; the fact that we are, whatever we are. The two aspects of the introduction are the one who introduces and the one who is introduced. The introducer or teacher is not introducing you to a body of knowledge, an accumulation of facts. They are introducing you to your ground which they can do because they inhabit their own ground which is not different from yours. If they are not at home in their own ground but only have ideas about it they will not be able to open the space of being for you. You will merely have learned a new 'spiritual' narrative and that is just more of the same but in a fancy package.

The one who is introduced is you. You are being introduced to yourself. That may sound ridiculous as you already know who you are. But as we looked before, this 'knowing who I am' is a construct, a little raft floating on the dark sea of unknowing. If you hold on to these ideas about yourself, you yourself will be ensuring that you do not find yourself. Truly you have to lose or rather loosen 'yourself' in order to find or be the wholeness of yourself.

The teacher has the fullness of the radiance of emptiness and the student has the fullness of concepts, emotions, expectations and so on. For the fullness of the ground to be received we have to be available – so the first and most important thing is to empty oneself of all that one is clinging to, building upon, protecting as if it were one's true identity. This is not so hard if one will simply give it a rest. Stop. The grasping mind is the ego's continuity. The ego strives ceaselessly to form itself from the happenstance of emergent experience: selecting this, rejecting that. And then, with the magic of self-deception, it fully inhabits this transient formation as an aspect of its eternal existence. So the ego is deeply into grasping, fusion, identification – these are its means of survival. But the whole cannot be encompassed within the part the ego takes to be the whole, the seemingly autonomous self.

Meditation is the arena within which the tricks of the ego come to light. By simply observing what is going on we come to see what we are up to. All that I am is vanishing in the very moment of its showing. For example, if I remember playing on the beach in Scotland when I was a child that memory seems to take me back there. It is as if I am traversing time. That is the comforting feeling-tone that gives me the sense that after all these years I am still me and am able to recall what happened to me. Something enduring is established. Truly? Actually what has occurred is the arising and passing of thoughts, feelings, sensations. Together they generate a feeling-tone which is also transient. The movement creates the illusion of stasis, of fixture, of moments enduring and transcending themselves.

The term illusion indicates something which appears to be the case yet is not, like a mirage on the road in front of you on a hot summer's day. We are taken in by the illusion, we are deluded by it, until we realise it is not what it seems to be. Waking up from the delusion that illusion is real is the means to freedom – even if at first it is a painful freedom because we have been so invested in the seeming reality of the illusion.

When we simply sit and observe the experiences that constitute the content of simply sitting we see directly that we are a flow of experiences, some of which appear as objects, some of which we take to be the subject. These experiences arise and pass as appearances devoid of real existence. None remain. And yet there is the undeniable fact that we are still here.

So if all that makes me 'me' is vanishing and yet 'I' am still here, who is the one who is still here? Having started to see that all phenomena are impermanent, are without solid essence or graspable substance, we are being introduced to the self-liberation of experience. We don't need to struggle to purify or empty our mind. It is self-emptying and self-purifying, and in fact is self-empty and self-pure.

With this opening of awareness of how experience actually is, we can work with the teacher to open to the inexpressible truth of the experiencer, the mind itself. This is the basis of direct introduction. When our mind is full of concepts that are relied on as valid in and of themselves our mind has no space to be introduced to itself. There is preoccupation, self-enclosure, foreclosure, darkness taken to be light, obscuration taken to be the transparency of self-evident truth. A student needs to be ripe. Some ripen in a day, others over a thousand lifetimes. The limit is one's own belief that hanging onto what one knows is vital. This mistaken belief hides us from ourselves. Let it go, for actually it's going anyway. But if you cling to the fantasy of your personal continuity as an entity with a defining essence – I am me because I am me – then you are calling night day.

The teacher tells us about the mind – more concepts. But the teacher is the openness of the mind. This is the transmission: to open to the presence of one who is present and who is not presenting themselves as being something. The openness of the teacher and the potential of the openness of the student meet as sky to sky: no boundary, no separation. This is the nowhere where the student finds themselves where they have always been. The mind is naked, not covered. All the content of the mind is fleeting and the nakedness of awareness is the clarity that illuminates all that occurs. The mind is fresh. It has no history, it has not developed through see xxii time or accumulated qualities or content through particular situations. Each moment is fresh, the showing of the ground, complete in itself just as it is. Each moment is new, offering a new beginning if we stay with the freshness and don't cover it with our habits and projections.

The mind is bright, shining, illuminating – all that occurs is the mind itself, showing itself, but not as its openness. The mind shows itself as its display, its radiance – which is everything we experience including all that we take to be ourselves. This is the mind but you can't define the mind on the basis of its display. The display in its ungraspable hereness and vitality shows the emergent potential of the mind yet the openness of the mind excludes definition and so we use metaphors and similes such as the mind is like the sky, awareness is like the sun.

This is the view. Staying with this view, being open to and as the ground, is the meditation. Not interrupting the flow of non-dual or integral energy is the activity. Finding oneself effortlessly at home in the inseparability of openness, clarity and emergence is the result.

Garab Dorje's second point is to not remain in doubt about this. To be in doubt is to be in two minds about something. On the one hand there is this opinion, on the other hand there is that opinion. This is unsettling. How can I be sure? There are so many sources of information, so many paths are presented – what should I believe, what should I follow? When these questions arise they are a sign that the first point has not been fully awakened to. Direct introduction is an unveiling of what is. And what is, just is. It is not something to believe in and it is not a path to be followed. The great completion is already complete. You are already complete so open to that completion and be with it. This is not something that the ego can do. Our egoic, self-referential sense of who we are will always tend towards closure, shape, definition, identity. The ego grasps at aspects of the content in order to give itself a filling, a substance. But the impermanent nature of this flow of content means that our ego is always insecure, no matter how seemingly confidently it asserts its identity. It is this fault line that feeds our doubt. We have all repeatedly identified with beliefs and activities which were later displaced by other objects of fascination. We let go of them and the space of identity filled with other new best friends.

If my mind is so fickle, if I am so changeable, how can I trust my new idea of myself? This doubt is helpful if we can see that it is a thought about other thoughts. Thoughts are unreliable by their very nature. If you build your life on thoughts you will always be busy trying to maintain your unstable construction. This is what is called samsara: wandering from one moment to the next in search of a stable refuge. Awakening to your actual being, to the concrete truth of being which is not generated out of concepts, is very different. This is letting go of all the old supports, all the hopes and fears, certainties and doubts that you had relied on.

Doubts feed the ego just as much as hopes and certainties. Yet you don't have to get rid of doubt; you don't have to decide against it and take a heroic stance of unshakable confidence. All the content of the mind is self-liberating. It will pass away by itself. So don't build your house on sand, nor water, nor fire, nor wind. The only stable habitation is space, the unchanging openness of the mind. 'Do not remain in doubt' means don't hang on to doubt as something useful. Let it go. Let everything go. Life will not end. The world will not stop. It is not all up to me. It is not my decision. It is what it is and no one hides that from me. I hide it from me by trying to fashion something secure out of the flotsam of events. Happenstance points to the hollow pretensions of the ego. Life disrupts plans. So when doubts and insecurities wrap themselves around our fragile sense of self, relax, allow what is to be what is and observe the passing of that entire matrix. We only remain in doubt by holding onto doubt.

The third point is to continue with this without seeking anything else. We live in modern complex cultures where new possibilities open every day. New technologies, job opportunities, relationships, foods, clothes, pathways to enjoyment and development are all readily available. There is always so much to be fascinated by. Me plus that might be better than me as I am – so why not try it? New experiences broaden the mind. This is generally true. But do they deepen it? Does more experience, more variety in life, let you stay with the actual revealer, the mind itself?

There is the experience, what I get, what happens to or for me. And there is the experiencer, who I take myself to be, my subjectivity, the one to and for whom experience happens. Both are impermanent in their content yet appear to be stable due to our concepts of self and other, self and events, self and environment. Each specific content vanishes yet the concepts always find new content to claim as their own. The hunger of the ego, its lack, leads it to see excess as a means of survival. Contentment and satisfaction are not enough. I need more, for the excitement of getting more, getting what I want, even getting what I don't want, gives me a sense of being alive. This is the root of the temptation of distraction, of turning away from what is already here towards what is elsewhere. The concrete is displaced by fantasy, imagining something better. We are caught by an idea because we are available to be caught. We are led astray because we are available to be led astray.

There is no need to apply the antidote of willpower and struggle. Such methods are unsustainable, for the flow of the energy of the mind never ceases and we easily forget what we had decided was essential. New possibilities manifest in each moment. This is the richness and diversity of life. And it is all self-liberating. Whatever comes, comes. Whatever goes, goes. Seeking to impose our puny will on the complexity of the immediacy of all that occurs moment by moment will not work. Nor will the complacency of ignoring diversity and sitting in the habitual, for this is also unsustainable and our smug sense of being able to manage life will end in tears. Be with what is and you will be grounded and centred in the openness of being. Moreover you will find that everything, everything, is the energy of the display, the effulgence of that openness of being. Being is impersonal, in that you cannot find it as something which you could claim as your own, yet it is nothing other than the basis of your presence, your aliveness, your life.

Being at home in the actuality of being has three aspects: openness, immediacy, and unlimited emergence. Openness is the emptiness of the mind, the inseparability of awareness and the infinite hospitality of the space of manifestation. 'Open' means not closed, not limited by boundaries, by definitions, by fixed capacity or by anything else. 'Empty' means free of presumed essence or substance. There is nothing to cling to – but then, of course, there is no one who needs to cling! Openness is naked, raw, fresh, relaxed – just here, always here, yet uncatchable. From this openness, with this openness, there is the immediacy, the clarity of presence. The open empty mind is full, full of colour, sound, sensation, life. This fullness is immediate, it happens all at once. Appearance is not a construct, it is not built up in stages but is effortlessly full, complete, perfectly just whatever it is as it is. This radiance of the mind is like the light streaming from the sun revealing everything instantly. Within this field of immediacy, the presence of the richness of the potential of the mind, there is the unique specificity of each moment of the emergence of energy. This is pervasive emergence free of limitation. It does not go from here to there but emerges everywhere. Each emergence arises straight from, yet without leaving, the ever-open ground.

These three aspects are our being. They have never been separate yet when we ignore openness, clarity is obscured and we are left as an illusory isolated self trying to stabilise unlimited emergence. This impossible task is the source of all the myriad forms of our hopes and fears and attempts to find lasting happiness. Letting go of this rather paranoid effort frees us to be who we have always been.

This is a book. So it is full of words. The function of the book is to offer words as flow, as massage, as mood, as gesture. We already know a lot about many things. Perhaps we don't need more building blocks for our self-creation. So instead may these words tickle your fancy and flow with you in the flow.

Ripples in the Flow

streams flowing in the flow
streams of movement, quick and slow
movement never ceasing
events a space are leasing
the fixed is flowing
the stable is going
you're not in a boat
so please stop rowing

THE HOW OF NOW

The how of now
could drive you insane
for now eludes how
and methods bring pain.

The mocker of effort
is always at play.
Whatever you grasp at
just slips away.

Neither coming nor going
it's always just here.
If you find yourself in it
there's nothing to fear.

So let go of method
for it's not up to you.
You have what you need;
it's happening as you.

How to be naked

All you have and
all you see
and all you take
yourself to be –
is only clothing.

Clothing can cover or
be the display
of the radiant source
forever in play.

Open and naked
you cannot be caught,
not by self nor by other
whether seeker or sought.

Fresh, raw and simple
our state is complete
though dressing's an option
for those whom we meet.

Sweet gift of nothing
this infinite field
the buddhas' own paradox
before which we yield.

Moment by moment
we arise in new forms
clothed in strange patterns
forever unborn.

It's fine as it is yet
what it is, it is not
Thinking won't get it –
it's a joke, it's a shock.

Naked is easy
so don't do a thing.
The clothes they come freely,
just see what life brings.

So how to be naked
is not something to know;
you're always uncovered
wherever you go.

Effort is wasteful
it muddies the water.
don't try to relax,
that's really improper!

It is what it is
as it always has been;
let the clothes slip away,
they were only a dream.

WIND BLOWS

Wind blows
leaves remain
wind rests
leaves fall

Autumn strangeness
shows me
myself

MIND FINDS ITSELF

Don't look in the manner of seeking something you've lost.

Don't look in the manner of a policeman trying to find a suspect.

But go like an ornithologist into the forest.

Find a peaceful place and sit quietly.

The bird is in the forest.

Trust this truth and don't move around restlessly.

Don't confuse yourself with busy thoughts of 'Is it here?', 'Is it there?'

With the movement of hopes and fears you will lose what can't be lost.

Just relax

For when the bird appears

Your mind is here.

It is not what you think it is.

ADVICE ON REFUGE

Stop taking refuge in your thoughts, feelings and sensations.
Stop taking refuge in your beliefs and assumptions.
Drop your belief in subject and object.
Take refuge in empty awareness
Whose clarity is everything as it is.
If you take refuge in the delusion that illusion is real
Confusion will continue effortlessly.

ALL THAT ARISES HAS NO ESSENCE

Each thought will pass, that is its way
Yet the awareness that has revealed the thought remains.
Awareness is like a mirror, thoughts are like reflections.
Reflections arise due to causes and conditions,
Without essence, they are fleeting and unreliable.
The mirror doesn't move yet reflections keep on arising.
If you move in response to the reflection
You yourself are just another reflection,
And will tumble on and on, wandering in samsara.
By not moving
See every movement is empty illusion.
This wisdom evokes compassion for all lost beings
Diligently erecting their hopes of permanence
On the groundless ground.
The true source of the busy builder is changeless space.
Everything else is the play of the mind.
Wonderful!

HERE IN THIS MOMENT

Here in this moment
There is movement.
It feels as if we are moving
Yet we are not moving:
Awareness never moves.
The world is moving
The body is moving,
Words are moving,
But our true being does not move.
In not moving it is always here,
So no need for a journey to find it.
Our true being is not hidden.
It's not behind us,
It's not in front of us,
No need to try to buy it,
No need to try to steal it,
It's just here with us
Where it has always been.

Playful display

Kuntu, always; Zangpo, good.
Always good.
The basis is vital emptiness.
Its field is unchanging clarity.
Its energy is precisely this.
Everything, everywhere, everytime good.
Everything always already good however it is,
Whether useful or useless,
Shining or dull.
No success no failure,
No winning no losing.
Allow whatever arises to take its place and then leave,
Appearing and disappearing in the manner of a dream.
Without self or essence
Each appearance the gift of space,
The flow of mind's energy
In playful display.

I'M A STRANGER HERE MYSELF

I'm a stranger here myself,
Being both strange and estranged,
Not quite at home except
In the space which is not
A territory, the space
Which is hospitable to
All strangers, all the strange
Who stray.
This space subverts the possibility
Of being estranged by its
Ease of offering the actuality
Of always already at-home-ness.

So where exactly is it that
I am the stranger, both strange
And estranged? Ah, it is here in this
Setting cut off from its own ground
By the tidal wave of thoughts,
Alienated only by the surplus of my
Own effulgence; creativity enveloping
Itself in itself. The isolated, apart, abject
Is but a fold in the unfolding flow
Of the myriad ways of being at home
As openness, field and specific moment.

RESTLESS

Everybody has stories of grief. We all have hassles and troubles in our lives. However from the point of view of buddhadharma these upsets are not the heart of the matter. These are like bubbles or froth on the surface, momentary disturbances generated by deeper structural faults. What really ails us is not being at peace in ourselves, not being who we truly are. In being alienated from ourselves we live as refugees, and refugees have a very hard time.

As a refugee you cannot settle in yourself, you are always wondering what is going to happen next. You have no stable basis nor any entitlement and you don't even have a passport. It is this very homelessness which is indicated when the texts say that we wander endlessly in samsara. A Tibetan word for sentient beings is 'dro wa', a traveller, somebody who is on the move. We are always chasing after one thing or another, hoping that the objects we find will provide a real refuge, a real home for us. Yet all situations arise and pass. We think we have found something or someplace or someone safe and secure and then ... something shifts ... and it has gone. This is always the case. Phenomena cannot provide true safety and security. This is not a punishment. It is just how life is when we have not awoken to how we actually are.

SPUME

Infinite spacious awareness and the gestures arising from it is primordial. Within the great theatre of the mind myriad dramas play themselves out. To see that this illusion is illusion is enlightenment itself. The games we play – being good, being bad, having hopes and having fears – are just frothing waves atop the ocean. Every phenomenon, everything that happens, good, bad, high, low, wanted, not wanted, is inseparable from our unborn mind. Like a dream, like a rainbow, this ungraspable life offers wonders without limit.

REFUGE

When we follow the buddhadharma we start our practice by taking refuge. We take refuge in the Buddha, the Dharma, the Sangha, and also in the guru, the meditation deities and the dakini goddesses. There are many different sites of refuge that we can turn to but the main point is to stop taking refuge in our own thoughts, in our own beliefs and assumptions. Who is the one who seeks refuge? Seeing that the seeker is an energy formation, a pattern revealed by our ever-still awareness, we have true refuge. But taking refuge in thoughts about who that one is will lead us astray. Lazy habitual reliance will cheat us again and again. If we take refuge in delusion, confusion will continue. So wake up to your lively freedom!

TRUE PEACE

True peace is not generated out of the qualities of the objects we possess, nor out of the qualities of the environments we inhabit, nor out of the qualities we take to be our own. True peace is a quality of refuge. When we recognise that our own mind is unborn awareness, that the space in which we move is the infinity of the limitless hospitality of the dharmadhatu, the realm of all the buddhas, and that everything we do and everything we encounter is the unborn compassion of the union of emptiness and awareness, then we can have true peace and grasping will be at an end.

LIFE IS ALREADY HERE

Relax and be present with yourself. This is not an active looking for something but a receptive availability to what is here. Without agenda, awareness is open to what is. No selection, no bias, no editing. Everything is as it is and we get it all as it is. The infinite moment is full and empty.

TRUST

Why be so busy? Perhaps you don't have to do so much. Good situations will vanish, for sure. Bad situations will vanish, for sure. Leave off planning. Life will happen as it will. As the children's rhyme says,

> Little Bo-Peep has lost her sheep
> And doesn't know where to find them.
> Leave them alone and they'll come home
> Wagging their tails behind them.

All the thoughts, all the experiences that can ever arise, go free by themselves. Just as the sheep come back to the home field in the evening so thoughts arise from emptiness and return to that home when their brief moment of display is over. Our life as it is is part of the flow of events. Our place in the world is revealed to us each day. We can work with this as neither masters nor slaves. We can allow our life to be as it is without anxious correction or disappointment. Familiar patterns will continue as long as their causal force. When that is gone they dissolve. We have already lived so many lives in this life. When a form dissolves, the potential from which it arose releases new forms. The clarity of the mind ceaselessly displays the flow of emergence, the transient patterning of its creative effulgence. Life goes on: walking, talking, eating, sleeping. Looking for substantial reliable essence-entities in the display leads to grief, while relaxed participative enjoyment in the flow brightens the heart and pleases others. As William Blake wrote,

> He who binds to himself a joy
> Does the winged life destroy
> He who kisses the joy as it flies
> Lives in eternity's sunrise.

It's a long road to here

Seeing you I felt trust and
An eagerness to advance
The way was open now and
I must take my chance.

Yet it's not that simple
For as you knew for a fact
The effort to arrive
Is what holds me back.

Aiming for enlightenment
And trying to be like you
Kept me anxious and striving
With ever more tasks to do.

I cheated myself
By ignoring illusion.
Life became all too real
With deepening confusion.

Having tried trying
Then tried giving up
I've given up trying
And given up giving up.

On the way to here
I was anything but free
For there is no need to travel
The path is simply to be.

CALMING MEDITATION

In the practice of basic calming meditation, also known as shine or shamatha, we focus our attention on a simple external object or on the flow of breath at our nostrils. We make a clear intention that this is the only thing we will focus on. Whenever our mind wanders off we gently bring it back to our point of focus. In this practice we employ a conscious focussing of our attention in order to separate ourselves from our enmeshment within the fleeting contents of our mind. With this intention, the thoughts, feelings and sensations that arise are re-categorised, shifted from 'interesting' to 'distracting'. We are extricating ourselves from our habitual tendency to fuse with, and then react to, the various phenomena which arise. The aim is to stand apart from the ever-changing flow of experience, to simplify our intention, and through that to find a calm space free of pre-occupation and distraction.

Some of the thoughts that arise for us may feel quite spacious as if they are expanding our horizons, yet because we are absorbed in them we can't see them clearly. Our encapsulation in each transitory moment creates a decontextualisation which has us jumping from the world of this moment to the world of the next moment. Then strangely, the very isolation of these moments of experience generates the illusion of continuity as we slip from one moment to the next. This is accompanied by an exhausting subliminal sense of fragmentation and the felt need to hold it all together. This responsibility generates an anxious tension which feeds our further involvement with and interest in whatever is occurring as we try to establish whatever threats or benefits might be found in each event.

In the mahayana buddhist analysis of the two truths this is called the state of impure relative truth. Within this dualistic mode of experiencing we have the sense of the existence of real subjects and objects. This view is described as impure because the subject takes itself to be strongly real and also takes the object as strongly real. This reified polarisation generates judgements and the distortions of the five poisons, the afflicted emotions of stupidity/assumption, desire/attachment, anger/aversion, pride and jealousy. Our experience tends to be pervaded by affective colouration, an emotional inflection which brings enrichment or distortion to what is actually going on. In this state it is very difficult for us to see a situation without immediately having an opinion, a reaction which comes to be the main sense of the situation we take away with us. The meditation practice of calming the mind helps us to learn how to listen, how to taste, how to touch, without filling the fresh space of experience with our habitual attitudes and assumptions.

The practice of calming disrupts our usual patterns by encouraging a concentration which is simple and straightforward. It doesn't have a complex agenda and it is not improved by passion or emotional enrichment. You don't concentrate better on your breath if you are angry or sad or desireful. In other situations you may feel that you are concentrating more when you are full of desire or rage, for then there is strong energetic fixation on your chosen object. If you are really annoyed with someone there is a kind of tunnel vision and aroused attention to detail and you know exactly what is what about the object of your anger or irritation. When you are focusing on something with an affective arousal you fill it with your projections. You think you are seeing it clearly but actually you are creating it out of your projections, out of what you are imputing to be the case for the object. However, this is very different from a calm, clear, concentration. With calm concentration the object is allowed to be itself without provoking the mind to busyness, to associations and amplifications.

The more we calm the mind and find ourselves less prone to being caught up in what is arising, we start to feel more spacious and can see the actual status of what occurs. We are both more separate from what is going on and more connected to what is going on. True connection is not based on merging but begins with perspective; we have to be separate in order to see. We don't see clearly with fusion and we also don't see clearly with avoidance. When we see clearly we enjoy the safety of not being an entity under attack. The ego pretends to be independent but is actually very easily influenced and hurt by circumstances. Our ego develops a wide range of defensive moves – none of which is very successful since the ego needs contact with the environment in order to exist. Our calm mind, in being less reactive, is able to let events occur and observe them with a mindful un-involved attention. As our focused attention generates a sense of calm our mind is less buffeted by the waves of hopes and fears.

Events, thoughts, feeling, sensations and so on continue to arise yet seem to have less and less to do with us. They don't get to us, control us or overwhelm us. Appearances occur as transient illusory forms moving within the space of our calm mind. Practicing in this way we come to dwell in what is termed the pure relative truth. Within this we still identify with the sense that, "I am here as a subject experiencing objects," but these objects are now more simple for we are not telling them what they are. We are not seeing them mediated through our concern for gain or loss – gain in terms of our desire, "What can I appropriate here," and loss in terms of the aversion that is generated by the fear that our certainty or security could be taken away. Becoming relaxed and spacious and welcoming all beings into that open equanimity is the general path of all the mahayana teachings including tantra.

JUST PASSING THROUGH

When we relax into open space, into the presence of the intrinsic purity of the heart of all the buddhas, our mind is here and the energy of our mind is here, inseparable in non-duality. When the open ground of the energy is present as us, all that arises is clarity, but when we are distracted by the sense of subject and object as real entities then all that arises is deluding, obscuring where we actually are. In dzogchen the prime way of dealing with this delusion is to simply bring our attention back onto and as the one who is having the experience. By doing this, our focused attention relaxes into its own ground, our unborn open awareness.

In our daily life we are often fused in experience, caught up in the flow of events as if actor and action were one. This manner of experience can feel pleasurable when the experience is one that we like, yet it lacks insight since we can't see what we are up to. When we practise calm focussing and then widen our attention to let it register the flow of experience, it is as if we separate from what is occurring and become able to observe it. This allows us to make more conscious choices but can also intensify our sense of being a separate subject, one who can know, plan and act.

However, our attention, as a quality or capacity of our individual identity, is not settled in itself since it needs an object to support its own existence. The ego requires contact with something other than itself and so our attention is still vulnerable to distraction, to being caught up in the flow of dualistic experience. The ego is a sequence of temporary formations which arise and vanish due to causes and conditions. As long as our identity is formed around being an individual ego self we will be conditioned by circumstances. Even if we practise calming the mind and ascend the levels of undisturbed concentration, this is a practice of making good causes to get good results. When the fuel is burned up our rocket returns to earth. We need to find a way of being responsive without getting lost. We need presence, space and availability without attachment or dependency. For when we see something that makes us happy, the one who is happy may feel truly and totally happy yet is inextricably a part of transient experience. This fact should be clear to us because if the next minute someone says something we don't like, our happy feeling soon fades. Yet when happy, our fixation on the intensity of the moment seems to seal us in a bubble. When that bubble bursts we are in the next bubble and then when that one bursts we are instantly, seamlessly in another. This creates both the illusion of a permanent knowable self and a lack of attention to the contradictions between the bubble moments, each of which is taken to be 'the real thing'.

However, in dzogchen, by neither merging with the experience nor struggling to stand apart from it and observe, we see that our attention is an aspect of the energy of our awareness. So we relax into our presence as the experiencer and staying with, in and as the experiencer we find ourselves in and as unborn open awareness.

In dzogchen this is illustrated by the example of a crystal ball. If you put a crystal ball on a green cloth it will show a green tint and if you put it on a red cloth it will show a red tint. The crystal ball itself is neither green nor red. In the moment when the ball looks green if you say, 'This is a green ball,' then that is mere delusion. The ball looks green but it isn't. Due to causes and conditions it appears as green but its actual quality is not green, its actual quality is transparent.

The truth of our mind is like this translucent ball, for it is as if happy things make us happy and sad things make us sad. Our open, insubstantial being is unobstructing and unobstructed. Due to causes and conditions we experience many different things; experiences arise as the interplay of subject and object displaying within the field of awareness. Not seeing that this is the case, we are caught in a dualistic arena in which we strongly identify with one polarity, myself, and have many thoughts about the other polarity, everything else. When we attach to the transient colourations of the crystal ball we experience the ceaseless movement of our life in samsara. The one who attaches is itself a colouration. How strange, how sad, that empty illusion should cause so much grief to beings who are themselves illusory.

In the Tibetan language sentient beings are often referred to as 'dro wa', beings who move hither and thither without rest. Yet, in fact, we, as our true being, are not moving at all. Our mind itself is relaxed, open and completely stable, yet displaying all manner of transient arisings, some seemingly 'outer', some seemingly 'inner'.

At each moment this particular pattern of transient arisings is all there is. Arising is inseparable from the ground and vanishes like a rainbow in the sky. Yet if we resist the fact of the dissolving of this specific subject formation and take ourselves to be a context-independent enduring essence then we are tossed from one bubble moment to the next. We ignore our open ground and illusory display and confuse and misdirect ourselves within the delusion of reification and its consequent self-justificatory narratives.

One of the qualities of ignorance is a sense of lostness and anxiety. In order to reassure ourselves we are always busy giving ourselves something to do. This activity generates our sense of self, constructing our identity out of the patterns of our likes and dislikes, our successes and failures. This is a truly vicious cycle: I ignore the open ground of my being and take myself to be the identity created in dialogue with others; this identity is insubstantial, contingent and unreliable and so I am constantly busy maintaining the edifice of myself; due to this I am preoccupied and lack the calm, open presence that would let me see the open ground of my being.

Busy focused mobilisation appears to guarantee our safety yet events disrupt our plans and the consequent nervous arousal blocks our relaxation. Our suffering seems to say, 'do more, do better, try harder' and this leads us further from the ever-present open door of here and now. Having been raised with the belief in striving, it can be difficult to trust that releasing and relaxing is the way home.

The Teacher

Chemchok Heruka Yab Yum

Roaring emptiness
Destroying delusion
Ferociously freeing us
With unborn love

A common Tibetan refuge prayer says, "*I take refuge in the Buddha, the best of all the two-footed creatures. I take refuge in the Dharma, which is peaceful and free from desire. I take refuge in the Sangha, the best assembly.*" My teacher used to say, "*The best of these is the Dharma because it is peaceful and free of desire. The Buddha wants you to get enlightened, the Sangha will try and help you get enlightened but Dharma doesn't want anything from you. Put your money on the Dharma!*" 'Free of desire' sounds very sweet. Dharma is just there. It is there whether you pick it up or whether you leave it alone. It is not going to feel insulted if you feel no interest in it. It is not going to feel exalted if you feel very interested in it. Dharma is just Dharma and that is a very good refuge because it is always there, open and without bias or membership cards. It always has the same taste so every time you practise Dharma you find the same focus and the same welcome. It's not like a couple-relationship where you speak with your partner and what you say changes their mood, which in turn changes you. Your job changes, your kids change, the weather changes. Everything changes except that which doesn't change. That which doesn't change is emptiness and openness. This is the actual meaning of Dharma.

My main teacher is the late Chimed Rigdzin Lama, also known as CR Lama. He was a married lama who lived with his family and, when I knew him well in India, he taught in a university. He was a great scholar, a very powerful person, and he was not at all holy. He was very ordinary in his way of life. His qualities showed themselves without his making special claims about himself. In the lineages of Tibetan Buddhism there are many different styles of practice. Some lineages display themselves as being very pure and holy; that is to say, they set themselves in the domain of the sacred and create a mood which is separate from ordinary life. When you encounter that kind of setting you have the opportunity to experience something which is not like ordinary existence. Such settings tend to be ritualised and choreographed so that everyone knows their place and what they are, and are not, allowed to do. My teacher was, however, very much in ordinary life. He was very fond of university politics, supporting his friends and attacking his enemies. This is not holy activity but Oh, so very pleasurable! For many years I was his secretary, and I had to write, on the basis of his special English, very insulting letters to important people. In order to enter his world I had to let go many of the assumptions I held about how to live in a proper way. In the end, in order to practise, we each have to find a style which is in harmony with the energy of our potential as it responds to each unique setting in which we find ourselves. Being in the mandala, or environment, that Rinpoche created was very disturbing for me, and yet it was also liberating. It opened the space to see that our world is indeed a construct of our beliefs and assumptions. Freeing ourselves from relative truth, from truth based on comparing and contrasting, involves a leap of faith. Encouragement to make this leap was Rinpoche's wondrous gift.

Guru is a word that has many derivations. A key one, my teacher told me, is linked to the Sanskrit word for cow. That's because if you eat a lot of beef you feel very heavy and the Guru is one heavy dude. Essentially, a Guru is somebody who gives a teaching that is designed to bring about a transformation or awakening. The Guru represents the unbroken lineage of transmission from the time of the Buddha. The key thing about a Guru is that they should have studied a lot and understood what they were studying. They should have then practised deeply what they had studied, and awoken to its truth. They should then be able to communicate that in a way which is impactful to people on every level, on the level of their body, their energy system, their feeling and their thinking. Through that they help to turn people, to tilt their gaze in such a way that they start to experience gaps in the flow of their assumptions. These gaps are the first taste of the space within which what is shows itself. That is the function of the Guru, and it can be performed with formality, with informality, or a mixture of both.

CR Lama told us that when he was a child he was recognised as a tulku, an incarnate lama, and so had to be visibly involved in the monastery rituals, sitting on a throne alongside the other high lamas. Whenever there was a public initiation, the village people and outsiders would come to receive it and at the end would make some offerings. The head lama would get many offerings, but even very young tulkus like CR Lama would sometimes get something. Usually they would be offered a white scarf called a khata, but it didn't always happen. CR Lama would be sitting there and a person would come up holding out a khata. If Rinpoche leant forward to receive the khata, but it wasn't for him, then he'd get hit on the back of the head by his teacher who was sitting next to him. You have to learn not to assume that something is for you until it is actually offered. But if someone is offering it to you, you could also get hit if you did not immediately respond to their gesture. Not holding back, not rushing forward – you have to be fully present, right here.

This is also the essential instruction for meditation. Why? Because our job is not to assume what other people, or even the contents of our own mind are going to do. We have to be present, open and aware. We respond if required. If not required we remain relaxed yet attentive. If we go off into a daydream or an expectation, we're not here. The land of concepts is a never-never land, a realm of make-believe. Much of what occurs there is fascinating, pulling us into fantasy construction which leads only to further fantasy. This is something we can observe in ourselves. Look and see how often we bring our expectations and our assumptions into the world and act as if they are going to be the case. If we have power, we can act to coerce the environment to fulfil our expectations for a while—but sooner or later the fantasy is unsustainable and we are left confused and disappointed. Being fresh means that moment by moment we are here with what is, not somewhere else with what might be.

When Chimed Rigdzin Rinpoche came from Tibet to India, he had the chance to have a very lovely little monastery in a place called Tsopema which is in the hills in Himachal Pradesh. The climate is very nice there, and the monastery is by a lake that is sacred to Padmasambhava. Perfect. He made a retreat there and got on very well with the local ruler, the King of Zahor, who became his sponsor. Rinpoche had a sweet photo of the King in evening dress wearing a bowtie and standing by his grand piano, which his wife, in a ball-gown, was playing. What a relaxed easy atmosphere, so he was tempted to remain. However, if you have a monastery you need money, and if you need money you have to be pleasing to sponsors. You must spend a lot of time talking nonsense to people who are not really going to do any practice but who want to be special. So what CR Lama did instead was to get a job in an Indian university and at the end of every month he got his salary. He was given a university house to live in and a clear contract to fulfil. He said that was a better situation to be in. Being at the mercy of other people's moods and whims is not auspicious for peace of mind.

The most important aspect of the transmission is the relationship with the teacher. The teacher is the site of emptiness and contact with that emptiness can fundamentally alter the basis of our 'being in the world'. We see the teacher function out of nothing, out of space, directly showing the spontaneity of the empty mind. This is how all things are. The teacher is the special one who demonstrates the specialness of the ordinary. This is the deep specialness of all-pervading emptiness.

When we see someone as being a great teacher, we can believe that they are a manifestation of the primordial ground. Although we see ourselves as ordinary beings, we are also manifestations of that ground. On the level of judgement and evaluation, we can say, "This person is high, this person is low" but in terms of our connection with the open ground source, all beings are completely the same. Staying relaxed and open to the ground reveals the effortless play of manifestation. Living this non-duality makes the world much more workable.

One of the first things that Chimed Rigdzin said to me was that there is no enlightenment-injection. There is no kind of Buddha-substance that you can get hold of and inject into your arm and space out. In engaging with the Dharma one moves into a play in which all one's own limitations, confusions and false understandings come to the surface. Learning to release one's reliance on deluding phenomena requires being present in the clarity of your own mind—no one can do this for you. We release delusion by opening to its emptiness. We have to become aware of and intimate with the contents of our mind—intimate without impregnation.

CR Lama often said to me that if he were to meet Padmasambhava, the first thing he would do would be to hit him. Why? Because if it's the true Padmasambhava, he has a light-body and so wouldn't mind. In fact, he might even be pleased that he had at least one disciple who was able to think for himself. If it wasn't the true Padmasambhava he'd run away pretty damned quick. So either way he, CR Lama, would be safe. Naivety is not a good basis for entering the Dharma. That does not mean we can't have faith or hope or trust, but it has to have a mature quality, seasoned with a bit of scepticism.

When I was living with my teacher I had a little room at the back of his house. The room was packed with lots of tin boxes full of paper, and it was very hot. There was a window with no glass but it had bars on it and I usually kept the shutters open. One day when I came back from the village I opened the padlock on the door, went inside, and saw a snake moving about. I went to see my teacher's wife and asked if she had a long stick to use to get this snake out of the room. My teacher came round and asked me what I was doing, because I was lying on the floor with the stick trying to chivvy the snake out of the corner. "I am trying to get rid of the snake," I said. "The only thing that is dangerous here is you!" he replied and walked off. It is like that... it is our own mind which is dangerous. There are many snakes in India but most of them are not at all dangerous. I was making a great song and dance for no reason.

Agitation is not bad in itself; the issue is our involvement in the agitation. When I was translating texts with my teacher in India we would work in his back courtyard. At that time he kept dogs on the roof and they were always barking. The house servant was very noisy, clanging her pots and pans. Rinpoche's wife would be shouting at the servant, the servant would be shouting back, and I would be writing out the translation ready for the typist. The typist was sitting next to me on the table working very fast. Whenever he had finished what was there, he would be sitting tapping his fingers. There were many activities happening in our rather chaotic environment and they were all valid. The key point is that we have a choice whether to be distracted or not. If we are waiting for the perfect conditions to come, we may have to wait a very long time.

All possible forms of experience arise within the spacious sphere of revelation. Where do they come from? They come from space itself, they are the forms of space. Space shows itself as these forms. Similarly the emptiness of the mind shows the forms of our various thoughts and feelings. Why does it show these different forms? When I asked my teacher that question he said, *"Well, when you meet Kuntuzangpo you ask him."* This means, *'Shut up, and look at your own mind.'* Some questions are stupid and it is not helpful to ask them. 'Why' is often a very dangerous word, because 'why' is often a sign of our intellectualising. It is helpful to ask who is the one who is asking the question. If it's Mr Smart Ass then it's probably not very useful to continue. If it's Mr Humble you might get somewhere since open enquiry without presupposition can lead us to the site of our simple awareness.

There can be difficulties for us if we feel we need to have proof before we decide on a teacher or a teaching. People do say, *"You should check out your teacher for twelve years before you make a decision."* but by then he might be dead. So, how do you know? I remember once when I was translating a text with CR Lama and I noticed that there was an inconsistency between the description in this text and another one we had worked on. I pointed this out to Rinpoche and he said, *"Who appointed you to inspect the dharma? Are you working for the CIA?"* This is the problem. Who am I to check out whether one text or the other is true? There is a time for checking and a time for faith. The intelligence of our intuition, the sweet quickness of the mind itself, is generally more reliable and useful than the conclusion we construct out of concepts. We are the grateful recipients of dharma and we have to just eat what is put in our bowl. *"But maybe it is the wrong thing."* Then that is our luck. But if we eat what we get we will experience directly the advantages and limitations of this situation. Test the situation by participation, observe your mind – now you have good evidence for your decision. If we stay in the realm of thinking about, judging and checking, then we remain the hub of the wheel of concepts. All the spokes come and meet in us as we compare and contrast and our ego remains the measure of all things.

SHADOWLANDS

Indwelling anxiety blossomed
Early for me, its perfume of mistrust
Pervading every experience.

The song of fear, preoccupation
And vengeance drowned out
The rhythms others moved to.

Having lost my footing in the world's
Dance I wandered
Alone, wary of all I met in the
Desert around me,
Needy and ill at ease.

Participation was partial,
Furtive, unsustainable
Desireful yet hopeless
Driven yet unsatisfied.

Distrust opens the shadowland
Where loneliness hides in fear and contempt
Alienated space appropriated
As home territory for the
Likes of me, who, fearing betrayal
And humiliation, betray life
By letting death kiss the bride.

Transcendent exits beckon the homeless
Promising victory away from the challenges of belonging
The rising sun called this
Abject rageful one to the fantasy of a new beginning.

Yet old burdens were carried within my blood,
My bones and highest aspirations;
The light of hope refracted
Through bitter assumptions scarcely recognised.

Of yourself, you said,
"I don't trust anyone, and
Number one, I don't
Trust myself."

I, faithful student, believed
You, and practised the higher mistrust
Because I trusted my interpretation
Of you.

Years passed in toil, in production
Of the holy, while sawdust filled my mouth.
Openness, space, love
Increased my bitterness as I struggled
To make sense of all that I could not
Allow. My own limits limited the
World as my banal self-focusing
Kept me blind, frustrated and evangelical.
I didn't get it.

I didn't get it
'cos you didn't give it.
I didn't get it
'cos I was unworthy.

That there was nothing to get,
Well, arousal kept that
Purely theoretical.
That we find what we are looking for
Is a well-known and painful fact.

Repeated pain exposed my yearning
For happiness to be mere surface.
The tears were not an accident
But marked arrival at the deeper goal.

Seeing the fractured basis of my self,
Seeing a ground too weak to build on
You kindly collapsed it for me.
Yet I, resisting the healing free-fall,
Clung to fragments and accused
You of abandonment.

I wanted to be reassured but
You were kinder than that.
As the fragments have cooled over
The years of wandering, they take
Their place in space as space,
As little rainbows, enjoyable
If not clung to.

You are gone. Not gone
Away but gone in the vanishing
Of the dialogic struggle, the
Endless puzzle. You are
Not other and so self
Comes home to the field it never left.
Holding you apart, making you special
Was just an other move in the game of
'Let's build a prison'.

Truth is intransitive, it
Transits no terrain, reaches nowhere,
relies on no-one.

Trust is, just is,
Infinite, alone,
The field welcoming everything.

Trust requires no faith or belief,
Is neither thought nor emotion:
The simple openness of the heart,
The infinite welcome being
Gives to appearance.

I was studying a long prayer on Sukhavati, the Western Paradise, written by a Kagyu lama. The purpose of the prayer is to make a basis for connection so that when you die you will be reborn in this blissful western paradise. The text describes beautifully how after Amitabha, the presiding buddha, dies he will be succeeded by Chenrezi and when Chenrezi dies he will be succeeded by Vajrapani. The prayer tells us how long each one will be the ruler of this beautiful buddha realm. Later I was working on another text which said something completely different about Chenrezi's future. It did not even mention that he would go to Sukhavati. I asked CR Lama how this could be? He said, *"Well, when you read this book, believe in this book. When you read that book, believe in that book. If you try to compare these books you will go crazy."* I think this is true. Faith and an open heart takes us deeper and wider than a critical reading.

Teachings which are special, statues that are special, teachers who are special, are only special in terms of our relationship with them. The question is whether we use that relationship in a helpful way or in an unhelpful way. We may use our connection to this perceived specialness to inflate our own ego, or we may use it to develop our devotion to the practice. The objective truth and subjective experience are rarely the same. From a buddhist point of view everything has the same root value because emptiness is the source of all. All sentient beings are the same in emptiness although their appearances are diverse. This is their true value and should be respected. All beings have buddha fully present in the potential of the ground of their being. If we bow to the guru, we should also bow to everyone else since it is to the buddha in the guru that we bow and not to their personality. Nothing is special yet everything is special. Qualities arise due to causes and conditions; they come and go. Seeing this we can relax and open to everything. Only the indestructible vajra openess never changes and so is truly reliable. It abides in the heart of all beings.

A key element to working with the changing circumstances of the world is to have the freedom to walk away. If you can't walk away from a situation then you are in collusion with its limitation. You're trapped. One of the best teachings I ever had from CR Lama was, *"Always get a return ticket."* Wherever you go, always have a return ticket. Rinpoche had many experiences of travelling to teach and this usually involved staying with people. Sometimes these people behaved very strangely towards him. At first, on the telephone they were, *"Oh please come, Rinpoche, oh please, Rinpoche, we will do everything for you."* But once he got there they would feed him the food they themselves liked to eat and were not very considerate of him. Having been trapped once in that situation in a foreign country and without a ticket home he decided never to be trapped again. *"If it's not beneficial to be there, then get out."* That's very important. Going under the power of distracted others rarely leads to anything useful.

My teacher often acted in ways which I found completely outrageous. I just couldn't understand his behaviour. He certainly saw a lot more possibilities to situations than I did. He could be extremely generous and kind, giving people money, time, care and attention, feeding the western waifs and strays who wandered around India, taking them into his house, being incredibly hospitable and courteous. He could also be extremely direct.

Once we travelled together to a conference in Benares. On arrival we got off the train with our luggage and our papers which were packed in a large tin trunk with handles at either end. Rinpoche summoned a porter who lifted the tin trunk onto his head and carried it out to a tonga, a horse-drawn taxi, parked at the station entrance. We were going to Sarnath, the place where the Buddha first taught the dharma. When we reached the tonga the porter asked for a lot of money, expecting us to bargain for the actual price, but my teacher said to him, *"I will never pay you this money for this work. I will not pay you here. Now we take these boxes back to the train. I will pay you there but I never pay you here because you are a liar and a cheat."* Then he said to me, *"Okay, help me lift this box back on to his head."* The porter leant down, holding his little red turban in place to receive the trunk. I held one handle and my teacher held the other handle. Suddenly Rinpoche lifted up his end and banged it down on the porter's head. Bang! The porter fell over. Then my teacher gave him all the money he had asked for, and we got into the tonga and drove off. What was all this about? I didn't understand at all. Rinpoche just said, *"Ah, these things happen."*

Later we went to the conference, and in the afternoon we walked around the stupa and Rinpoche gave a lot of money to all the beggars there. Life with him was like that. He had a range of activities that were very difficult for me to understand. I wanted him to be a 'good' lama, according to my criteria, but my templates for right and wrong could not encompass how he was. His disruption of my assumptions was often confusing and evoked many conflicting emotions in me. Trying to make sense of him, to sort out what was going on, was gradually revealed to be a waste of time. He was what he was—direct, fearless, shameless, right at the heart of the situation. Analysing it only put me on the outside, judging and drowning in concepts.

As I learned to let him be him, I was able, at least a little, to let myself be me. As ripples in the flow of life, the 'meaning' is in the being here. Why he did what he did, I don't know. Anyway, he did it.

Nowadays there is a great cult of happiness and one Buddhist monk is even referred to in the media as 'the happiest man in the world'... but is this the point of life? CR Lama was often not happy, he was often in a bad mood and when he was in a bad mood he didn't keep it to himself; he compassionately shared it with everyone else! He lived in his practice. He wasn't blocking or editing or being artificial. He was working with the manifestation of the energy of his life as it arose. It would have been easier for us had he been polite and pleasant all the time, because then life would have been relaxed and free of friction. Rinpoche, however, used to bang into everyone. In fact, he delighted in banging into people as if to say, *"Don't pretend. Nothing is gained by pretending to be other than you are. Don't play at being better than you are, happier than you are. Don't make yourself false."* Of course in the outer world, it can seem necessary to behave in a nice way, and at social events he could be very charming to everybody. This was how he worked with their limitations: for his students it was different.

There is a short praise verse to Padmasambhava that he liked very much. It begins Ma Choe Troe Dral Lama Choe Kyi Ku: the dharmakaya lama is free of artificiality and fantasy construction. This is exactly the quality of CR Lama that I am describing. It means being open and letting the play of illusory appearance present itself through you. Being part of the drama of your own existence, you are touched and moved without ever being touched and moved. Intrinsic openness is indestructible.

Although our true actual presence is ever-open, suddenly, for no particular reason, we are caught by a thought. Being caught by the thought, we come into 'existence' as the illusion of 'I, me, myself'. This is not due to a curse, it is not the whim of a God, nor is it a punishment. It is just a moment in which the spontaneous effortless self-liberation of phenomena seems to experience a hiatus. There is a self-reflexive pulse, and an idea arises which is empty and fleeting, yet which is somehow 'sticky'. It seems to attach itself to another idea and then a chain of linking thoughts appears to hide the openness of presence in the way that minute droplets link to form clouds which seem to block out the sky.

My teacher explained to me that this slippage and attachment is like a drunk man falling down the stairs. He gets to the bottom and "Uh??" First there is disorientation and then thoughts arise that seem to provide reassurance. Due to relying on them he does not directly see where he is, relax and get his actual bearings. Instead he starts to invent ideas about where he is. Because the intrinsic presence of actuality is lost sight of in the effort to make sense of things, he faces the unending question, "What is going on?" He anxiously tries to fill the gap created by this question and so lives in a stream of answers, each of which quickly vanishes leaving the gap exposed again. The more these thoughts are taken seriously, the more they develop and increase the sense of 'I am me and you are you', intensifying dualistic separation. On the basis of this we take the illusory sense of self and other to be substantially real, and this delusion activates the perpetual motion-machine of karma.

Rinpoche said to me that by rubbing butter into leather we can make it soft, but if we use leather skins for storing butter then after a time the leather dries up and becomes hard and brittle. In the same way, if we make ourselves like a leather container and store the dharma inside without using it, we will become hard and brittle. We become experts who can use the words of dharma, but the actual richness of the dharma, the butter of it, doesn't soften us. We have to rub the dharma into our skins and into our hearts by giving ourselves fully to our daily practice.

While I was living with CR Lama in Shantiniketan there was a woman who had once taught in the university and who had become disturbed and was sometimes quite wild. Her family found this very difficult because educated Bengali society is very proper and somewhat uptight. Once when she was in a disturbed state and vulnerable, Rinpoche's wife wanted to bring her to live in our house. However he told her, "*You bring her in, you look after her! If you have the time and the energy to look after a mad woman in this house where you have four children, three dogs, and my students, then enjoy it! But me, I am not involved. So think carefully. If she does come then don't ask me to tell her to leave!*" Of course she didn't bring the woman to the house. It was a kind idea but the reality of bringing somebody who is very disturbed into your house when you are already over-stretched is unhelpful. That would be compassion without wisdom. We need to work with circumstances and that includes the current state of our own capacity.

CR Lama frequently said to me, "*Don't mix your food with your shit.*" This explains a lot. Food goes in one hole and shit comes out another hole. If you are a good farmer you can take your shit and spread it on the field to make more food grow, but you don't want to mix them directly. Our food is our direct presence, the absolute simplicity of being. It is not being this nor is it being that; it is not being big nor is it being small; it is not being male nor being female. Just being, simply being, pure being, reveals itself through being this and that. The being 'this and that' is the energy, the manifestation of the ground of being which is always open. The ground and its manifestation are not two and they are not one. They are non-dual, intimate in the way a mirror and the reflection within it are intimate. Because we live in duality and think in terms of this and that, we separate them in our mind and then, because they are so close together, we mix them up and live in confusion.

CR Lama used to say, *"There is nothing special."* Nothing is special, everything is the same. This is Kuntuzangpo, always good, everywhere good, everything good. Sometimes we feel that we receive a special message, something really important, like a vision or dream, or that we have some special purpose to our life. This may indeed be true, but if you believe it, it will cheat you. If it's special it will be special by itself, you don't need to invest in it in any way or build upon it.

CR Lama told me that the best practitioners of dharma are somewhat simple and stupid. Their minds are not busy all the time. They don't have a sense of mastery, or feel that they have to be in charge, and so they just do the practice. We can be too smart for our own good. We can be ahead of ourselves. If we find ourselves in that situation we have to slow down and just be with ourselves, be as ourselves. This means listening to how we are. If we attend to ourselves we will find a lot of direct instruction, out of our own embodiment, about how to live our lives. This frees us from unnecessary and unhelpful involvement in the turbulence of transient events.

After I had finished doing my first set of prostrations, I told to my teacher, *"I finished my prostrations."* He said: *"Oh, are you tired?"* "Yes," I answered. *"Good,"* he replied, *"Now look at your mind."* Then he explained that the only function of doing prostrations is to get tired, which is why you should do a lot at once. Doing a hundred a day is not so helpful. You should do a lot till you are completely exhausted, and then you sit and be with your mind. However it depends on the teacher. Some teachers may say: *"Each day you can do one hundred of each of the five parts of the preliminary practice and after three years or so it will all be completed."* We can focus on the virtue of doing practice or we can use it to reveal our mind.

X One of the functions of the teacher is not to be very interested in you. You are not as fascinating as you think.

My teacher described how when he was young he had studied medicine with one of his uncles. The students were set the task of going out and bringing back all the things that were of no use as medicine. It was explained to them that this was so that they would recognise what was not helpful. The students went and they looked all over the hills and brought back various plants. CR Lama, however, came back with nothing. His uncle said, *"Exactly. Everything is medicine. If you know what to do, the stones, the plants, water from different pools, everything is medicine. Nothing is unhelpful."* This is at the heart of our dharma practice. We try to see that every aspect of ourselves is useful. Even our anger is useful. Once we start to see things in this way, compassion takes on a very different meaning. When what we would normally see as our negative tendencies are appreciated as actually being useful, then we start to see that the negative tendencies of other people are also very useful. Rather than helping other people to change how they are, the actual focus of compassion shifts to helping people to see what they're up to and to see who it is who is up to it.

F aith is a way of opening and it involves seeing if we are living in ways which restrict our potential. Although we can learn mudras, the practice is not particularly about whether we can make the mudra in the right way or not. It is about coming into a sense of the body as movement, as lyrical movement. We could all see this with CR Lama. He was very beautiful in the movement of his body. He had a very clear and powerful aesthetic sensibility. Often he might wear very strange clothes. Somebody would give him some funny orange-coloured garment and he would wear it. I remember in Wales, he used to wear a peach nylon negligée. He also bought a pink satin quilted lady's dressing gown that he liked to wear. He always looked very beautiful because he was completely at home in himself. He wasn't thinking, *"Oh, what do people think of me from the outside?"* He was just at home in himself, *"Oh, I like this!"*

C R Lama often reminded us, *"Don't leave this life empty-handed. Don't waste your time. Value yourself. Do the practice. Have faith in Padmasambhava."* The particular teaching of CR Lama was that you should pray one-pointedly to Padmasambhava. If you pray with full faith, without any doubt, all the energy systems of the body will meet in your heart. Your mind will become empty and in that moment you can recognise your intrinsic being.

A ll the buddhas and bodhisattvas have made a fundamental commitment to help us. My teacher said that if we pray to the Buddha, he will definitely help us. Have no doubt about that. Our texts repeatedly say that doubt is a great limitation since it brings us into thinking about something rather than entering direct experience. Doubt cuts the rainbow bridge between our heart and the hearts of all the Buddhas.

Do we practise dharma to benefit everyone or to benefit people who are very close to us? CR Lama used to say, *"There is no virtue in the family,"* by which he meant that to take care of your family is not a virtuous act because your family is an aspect of yourself; they are your world. Taking care of your children is, in some way, taking care of yourself. However to take care of someone else's children is a different matter because duty, obligation and family identification are not present, and you are having to step over the boundary of self-interest to be available to someone who is truly other. In the mahayana path a lot of time is spent reflecting on how we can become more aware of other people, more thoughtful about them, more empathically attuned with them. Even then we need to ask ourselves, *"What is my self-interest in helping this person."* Only when there is no self-interest does it become an altruistic gesture.

CR Lama used to say, *"If a yogi has sex in the middle of the road, no-one will notice. However, if ordinary people have sex in the bushes everyone is staring at them."* He himself was often quite shameless, unconcerned whether he was rude or not. He wasn't being self-indulgent or aiming to get away with doing bad things on account of being a lama. Rather, he was living exactly in the moment, in impermanence, in the self-liberation of all phenomena – this is the space of ungraspable presence.

CR Lama lived in a small university town in India. Actually it was smaller than a town, more like a village. He didn't like to walk at all, so there were always rickshaws waiting outside the house. He used to take a rickshaw to work, and sometimes he would go out just in his lungi, a short wrap-around cloth, and a tee-shirt. His wife would come out and shout at him, *"Oh, you can't go to work like that. Shame on you! What are you doing?"* And he would reply, *"Who do you think is going to work, CR Lama or CR Lama's clothes?"* If you rest in open clarity then anything and every-thing is okay. But once you start to bind yourself to what other people might think of you then, since there are a lot of people with a lot of differ-ent thoughts, you will always be busy trying to second guess what they expect of you and worrying about whether you fit their expectations.

CR Lama used to say that he didn't like people with broken hands, meaning, people who only talked. He liked people who would do things. If something needs doing, you do it and then it is done. In that way life is very simple. Time-wasting binds us to linear time. If you don't do something when it needs to be done then you have got to remember that you haven't done it. You put it into the future but now you can't be fully in the present because you have to remember to do in the future the thing that belongs in the past!

The basis of ethics in the practice of dzogchen is to not be carried away by identification and interpretative structures but to stay with the immediate freshness of the living situation. In that way, we can see that all manifestations are the energy of the ground, self-arising and self-liberating. Once when CR Lama was in retreat in Tsopema in north India a thief came to the house and took many precious possessions including his wife's jewellery. His wife wanted him to go to the police, but he said, *"Don't you believe in karma? Karma will punish the thief. It is not my job. Let it go."* That is a very open response to the situation. Otherwise we have hopes and fears and become involved in sending someone to prison—all because we want 'justice'. However, if we understand karma, if somebody robs us, this is the result of some previous action by ourselves. Who are the criminals? Who are the bad guys? It is impossible to discriminate. So, seeing that every situation is complex and simultaneously simple in its intrinsic purity, stay relaxed and open.

In the Tibetan tradition there are mantras for everything. There are mantras for the fireplace, for making beer, for protecting the beer from going off. They have mantras for finding lost sheep and they have other mantras for finding lost cows. This is a fact. When I was first learning Tibetan I went to Bodhgaya. They used to sell lots of Tibetan books around the main temple and I bought some books and took them back to my teacher and said, *"Look I have brought back all these wonderful books. Which one should I study."* He looked through them and said, *"Well this one here is for someone who has lost their cow. This is the prayer and the mantra you have to say to bring back the cow."* Now clearly in Tibet that was very important. You need to have milk and for that you need a cow and if it gets lost then that is a problem. If you believe that the thing that can protect you in life is the dharma then naturally the person you turn to for help is the lama. If the lama has a book with a prayer in it that he can read then the lama will feel confident that he is doing something helpful in the name of the Buddha to help this man find his cow. The man will be grateful; he will get his cow back and offer some of the milk or butter. This is an interlocking system of values. Some of the values are worldly and some are spiritual and they operate together. The prayer for finding the lost cow is niched within a symbolic field and has a useful purpose in that it helps the dharma to be supported by and to be part of that culture. However for we westerners who are practising to develop wisdom and compassion, and who do not have cows, these prayers are not so useful. We each have to start by looking at our own situation. This will indicate what kind of dharma practice is required.

There is no limit to the creativity of the mind. So many ideas and inventions, both good and bad, arise due to causes and conditions. Everything that arises for us is the illusory movement of the energy of the mind which is intrinsically empty. The danger for us is that we start to believe that all these possible arisings are strongly real and this condemns us to the seeming necessity of endless activity. In terms of practice, you actually need only one tantric practice, one deity. You pray to the deity, you dissolve with the deity, you go into emptiness and you arise from that with clarity. One is enough.

There is a saying in Tibet, *"In India, people do one practice and get enlightened. In Tibet we do a hundred practices and nobody gets enlightened."* They have this saying because they have so much dharma, and all of it is valuable. We need to take responsibility for our dharma practice and not lose sight of our truest intention.

C R Lama said of himself, *"I am liar number one and cheater number one."* This is a very important teaching. Once you know how you lie to yourself, once you know how you cheat yourself, you have the beginning of true practice. When we sit in meditation we see the many ways in which we cheat ourself. There are many, many thoughts which easily catch us, and many ways in which we abandon ourselves into whatever is arising. The basis of practice is to be honest with ourselves and to work with whatever occurs without complacency or blame. But if you think you are a 'holy buddhist practitioner' who has 'got' something, you are very likely to fall asleep in this assumption. Then the freshness of a moment of understanding becomes just a memory that you use to console yourself. Investigating how we deceive ourselves is very important. It is one thing to say, *"Now I recognise this I won't do it again,"* but that intention isn't going to last for very long since our habits will be back again soon. Being rigid is not the point; softness is always much better. Be very close to your experience and kind to yourself in your confusion and lostness, and bring yourself gently back into the heart of the practice.

I diot compassion, as referred to by CR Lama, means indulging in vibrating at other people's distress. True and useful compassion, nyingje in Tibetan, means to have a noble mind. A noble mind is a mind with dignity. When people become caught up in their suffering they often lose their dignity. They become helpless and useless and want to be saved. The actual way to help people is to bring them back to their dignity. If you encourage somebody to be a victim, dependent, useless and hopeless, this is to insult the actual basis of their existence, their own ever pure source.

Y ou can find thousands of books on dzogchen. So how come the tradition which began with Garab Dorje's three short pithy statements gave rise to tens of thousands of books? Because people like conceptual elaboration. People just don't leave well alone. I was lucky that CR Lama didn't like to talk very much and always said everything in a very simple way. He said, *"Depth and light, open, empty awareness. This is enough. With this you'll see the truth of your own mind. This is not very difficult. Here is what you do. Stay relaxed and open with whatever occurs. Don't do anything else. Now don't get lost!"* There is nothing more than this. But if you don't get it then there are plenty of techniques you can use to pass the time.

CR Lama often explained that, *"The buddhadharma has one taste. In our Nyingma lineages we have nine different vehicles, but they are not in contradiction; they all go in the same direction. Once we understand the five skandhas, it is easier to understand emptiness. Once we understand emptiness, it is easier to understand tantric transformation. Once we understand tantric transformation, it is easier to understand primordial purity."* This is because they all point to the same thing, that the mind is chief. The mind creates samsara and the mind creates nirvana, yet the mind has never been created.

CR lama was explaining to me Patrul Rinpoche's lines at the end of a brief text on dzogchen, *"However it is a waste not to show these instructions to those who will guard them as their life, and, practising the essential meaning, will strive to gain buddhahood on one lifetime,"* which he said were rather political. In Tibet there was a strong tradition of not making dzogchen teachings publicly available. There were many small family lineages of dzogchen practice. Dzogchen instructions would be passed on inside the family. In a big monastery, however, the instructions would often not be available to the ordinary monks, and certainly not to lay people. Patrul Rinpoche, however, liked to make teachings available to everyone. These lines indicate that it is waste of dharma if you don't help people who can learn. Many teachings are called very secret, and are sealed with protective symbols. But against whom are they to be protected? Pure motivation and impure motivation are not so easily distinguished. We meet together to practise and learn, and our faults and limitations come along too. So we each have to endeavour to become the ones who will guard the teachings as our own lives. This is the basis for transmitting the dharma.

W hen I was a child I used to fight with my brother. Two brothers, two children born from the same mother. My mother used to look at us fighting and say, *"I don't understand why you are always fighting!"* The great mother, Prajnaparamita, emptiness herself, the mother of all the buddhas, gives rise to a lot of children, but these children don't always like each other either. When you sit in meditation and thoughts of, *"I like this; I don't like that"* arise, this is the conflicted play of the mind's offspring. This is the energy of the mind showing the form of competition, rivalry, envy and so on. Why is it like that? When I used to ask my teacher CR Lama questions like this he would say, *"Well, when you get to Zangdopalri and meet Padmasambhava, then that can be your first question."* Which is to say, *"Keep quiet, look in your own mind and don't bother me with your conceptual nonsense."*

O ne of my teachers, Chatral Sangye Dorje Rinpoche explained the function of the teacher in this way. There are two brothers, one is asleep in bed having a nightmare and the other is lying awake beside him. The one who is sleeping is imagining that all kinds of terrible things are happening, but the other brother can see that he is actually asleep, safe in his own bed. Our teacher, our happily awake brother, sees us lost in our dreams and nightmares and encourages us to awaken. But we are attached to our lostness, even to our nightmares or addictions, which though terrible are perversely reassuring. When we wake up, we wake up where we are, safe in bed. We find we haven't been anywhere else, except in our delusion. Similarly awareness itself has never been contaminated, or mixed up with, or confused by, any of the events of our life. All the events of our life so far have come and gone. When we remember them, it is as if they come back to us and we can tell some stories about them, but we can't go back into the past. All that was, vanishes, so be awake to whatever is occurring and then there will be no more nightmares.

When I met my teacher CR Lama, the very first thing he told me was, *"The buddha is not a nice man."* This is very helpful. The buddha is not a nice man. The buddha is the unborn dharmakaya. Buddha is inseparable from the open space of the dharmadhatu. The buddha is not a person or a thing. Buddha is not nice nor not-nice. Buddha is not anything familiar. Buddha is emptiness, the radiance of emptiness, the inseparability of the sun and the clear blue sky. The clear blue sky symbolises the open, luminous expanse revealed by awareness within which all manifestation is occurring. The buddha is everything yet we keep relying on our partiality and our judgements, *"But I don't want these anxious thoughts in my mind!"* Who says that? A thought-sequence. One thought evokes or calls into being another thought. Each of these thoughts sets off another and another and another out of which we form our sense of ourselves and our world. Our ego-self is in fact just this concatenation, this linked sequence of patterning. Our life evolves as shifting patterns devoid of self-substance, for our life is the luminous display of the mind. The one who sees this is buddha – so much more than being a nice man. Temples are full of very beautiful shiny statues and seeing them can give us the sense that our buddha-essence is likewise very bright and shiny. Yes, our mind's true presence is radiant – but this radiance is not just warm, bright, primary colours. All colours spread from it and that means the greys, browns, and blacks as well. Our good thoughts and moods and our bad thoughts and moods are equally the radiant expression of the unborn mind.

I did a retreat in Tso Pema engaging in many kinds of practice including prostrations. At the end of the retreat I told my teacher all that I had done. Referring to the prostrations, he asked me, *"Why did you bother?"* I said, *"I thought I was meant to do them."* And he said, *"Oh yes, you thought you had to."* I replied, *"Well, it does say in the text that we have to do that."* My teacher then said, *"But did you ask yourself if it was doing you any good? What is the point of me teaching you dzogchen if you want to be stupid?"* So, in the end it is up to us. All the methods are good but only we live in our own skin.

A key instruction I received from my root teacher, is, *"Whenever you have a problem in meditation, don't apply any antidote. Stay exactly where the problem is."* We always want to do something. Why? Because we just want to do something. Control your breathing. Do kumbhaka. Do pranayama. *"Okay, now I feel better."* Of course you feel better, because you went from something bad to something good. *"Oh! Bad is not the same as good? Hm!"* This is called 'duality'. Hm... You have gone from one kind of shit-heap into another kind of shit-heap, except this one tastes like chocolate. That's the only difference. This is very important because the fantasy of choice and control will condemn you to wander in samsara. The ego defines itself by the choices it makes but unborn awareness makes no choices. It simply reveals the display of its own energy – one form of which is our ego busy making choices.

Rinpoche often used the image of a ring and a hook to illustrate the nature of the student-teacher connection. He frequently said that it was important to develop a strong ring of faith so that the hook of the guru's blessing and compassion could catch that ring. In order that the vital life of the lineage continues, the transmission has to occur through the meeting of love and devotion.

The first teachings I had from my teacher were to eat regularly and sleep regularly. These structured behaviours help our embodied system to calm down and be available to respond to circumstances. He explained that there are four activities for the yogi: walking, sitting, eating and sleeping. When you are tired, sleep, when you are hungry, eat. It is not so complicated.

My teacher frequently told me to make life as easy as possible, to do things the quick way. This is very helpful. Life does not have to be hard.

We see that work is indeed laborious yet we become inured to it. We learn to knuckle down and just get on with it. There's a sense of drudgery. But actually work is simply the flow of energy. Since energy is always flowing and we are always within that flow as part of it, once we find the ley line of work, once we get in the rhythm of it, we are carried by the flow of the energy of the world. Work is difficult only when we can't find the rhythm. The purpose of all the wisdom teachings in Buddhism, the teachings focussed on emptiness, is to loosen the heaviness, the consolidating function of our mind, so that we become light and delicate and start to feel the possibilities of movement. Then compassion flows as required, for compassion is the capacity to be with others, to reach and make a connection with them in as many ways as possible according to the situation.

Mahamudra is sometimes translated as 'great seal'. Here is one explanation I got from CR Lama. In Tibet when the king wrote an official letter, a formal seal would be attached to it. This was also done in medieval Europe, with a seal being pressed down on hot wax, leaving its impression on the wax. When the document is sealed in this way, nobody should change it, nobody should interfere with it. When our mind is sealed in non-duality there is nothing to be added, nothing to be subtracted – it is just as it is. This is what is meant by the 'great seal'.

CR Lama said that if you have a tree that you want to get rid of, you may start by picking off all the leaves. It takes a long time to take off each leaf, and by the time you have finished with the leaves on one side they are starting to grow back again on the other side. So it's much better to cut the root. You cut the root and the tree dies. The ego and all its activities are planted in concepts. Ego and the concepts or assumptions reinforce each other. We cannot stop the flow of concepts – and indeed they are part of the work of compassion – but what we can do is to cut the root of the tree of ego. The sharp knife of emptiness slices up reification and the deluded sense of individual essence. The tree dissolves, liberating the energy of life to be available for the common good.

Tired of myself and longing for you

Caught by a thought
like a fish in a net
I am born as one dragged
by a rope round the neck.

Before in the stillness,
the wide open space,
presence is given,
relaxed in its place.

Its place is pervasive
without having to move
alive and refreshing
with nothing to prove.

But caught by the thought
I lose my own ground
and grasping for more
mere illusion is found.

I feel I exist
since I seem to be real
yet nothing is stable
for the truth is concealed.

I'm a subject, I'm an object
yet neither remains.
it exhausts me creating
these sources of pain.

Oh, net of illusion
please leave me alone –
but in taking you seriously
I make you my home.

Turning and searching
I never can find
the one taste I'm lacking -
my own peace of mind.

Give me a break!
I scream at myself
yet it's me who picks up
the next thought from the shelf.

Row upon row
offering endless delusion
the constituents of self
bring only confusion.

The web is woven by
my struggle for more
yet the balm that I seek
from the source always pours.

Not self and not other
but the space in between,
this small gap is infinite
the ground of all dreams.

So many kind teachers
have pointed the way
back home to the source
yet I choose to stray.

I play with my toys
bored, lonely and sad.
I feel cheated by others
whom I then make bad.

Subject and object are
weaving their spell.
Shut up! Enough!
I'm falling in hell.

Sinking in sadness
I remember your face
my heart fills with tears
for I've turned from your grace.

I know all the words
but my heart is like stone
so busy with good works
I avoid being alone.

Always engaged and
caught up in stuff
it may be called 'dharma'
but it's just ego's puff.

Due to your kindness
I know where's the door
to the open expanse
that you showed me before.

I'm tired of myself
so it's time to begin
to relax and to open
letting everything in.

We are never apart
though I keep you at bay
you're here in my heart
yet I ignore what you say.

You always forgive me
'It's just movement in play'
but I'm guilty and serious
with my fine feet of clay.

Applying the practice
is being close to you
you've made it so easy
yet it's the last thing I do.

So I'll sit still for a moment
and rest in this space
and find myself mirrored
in your smiling face.

You've given me gold
but I'm searching for lead
it feels like a problem
that's stuck in my head.

I can find no solution
since the problem's not real
the snake that's a rope
gives a bite you can't heal.

I'm lost and confused
and I feel so alone
while living within
your mandala home.

So full of myself
I've no space to receive;
thought's endless production
is just a disease.

I call out to you
as an object apart
it's my own dualism
that enfolds me in dark.

You're here and you're smiling
and now I'm here too
released in the out-breath
thoughts dissolve in the view.

There's nothing between us
we're both like the sky
nothing can touch us
as appearances float by.

Filled up with nothing
I'm wide open space
neither lack nor excess
can leave any trace.

Oh what a struggle
and with no need at all
you've been ready and waiting
yet I couldn't call.

Always alone and
forever complete
at peace and content
at your lotus feet.

ANXIETY

Samsara is a state of anxiety. In samsara subject and object are separated, and we find ourselves strongly identified with the subject. The subject needs something from the object and yet it is fearful of the object. Desire and aversion, love and hate arise as sequential twins. As the Buddha said, friends become enemies and enemies become friends. Subject and object, self and other are co-emergent and mutually influencing. Neither is a self-existing entity. They emerge as patterns in the flow. The instability and unreliability of subject and object leads to anxiety and this is increased when we wish them to be other than that instability and unreliability. When we accept their dynamic unfolding, the door opens to seeing that they are, in fact, the energy of the open ground of being.

In the course of our lives, many doors have appeared in front of each of us offering new opportunities and new possibilities. Yet because of doubts, confusion and feelings of anxiety, we didn't go through these doors. It's helpful to reflect on this and see the power that our identification with limiting thoughts has to determine the patterning of our identity. An impermanent thought, in claiming to define a situation as finite and permanent, obscures the sole permanent situation, the unchanging openness of our awareness.

Control

F rom the point of view of dzogchen, collaboration and participation are much more important than dominance and control. That is to say, we relax and find ourselves within the field of our participation. The world reveals itself as we reveal ourselves – nothing is fixed and everything moves together. The field of experience is responsive yet will always slip out of our attempts at total control. The one who wants control is the one who is already in duality.

E go is concerned with mastery and so it asserts its separation from the field of experience and occupies itself with deciding whether it will engage or not—yet either way it is always already participating.

T o awaken to and abide within and as one's own open ground involves leaving the matrix of control and awakening as relaxed spaciousness. The spacious mind is not other than whatever is occurring. Then, with nothing to defend, there is no basis for hopes and fears. This equanimity brings deep tolerance. The fact that some people don't like us and some people do like us is just how it is – so we can relax and work with circumstances, with the transient events which constitute our experience.

The problem is never with the object. The answer is never with the object. The problem and the answer are always with the mind. The problem is the mind that wants to control and interfere and make 'things' the way we want them to be. The answer is the mind that relaxes and trusts the emptiness of the flow of self-liberating experience.

It is very important not to feel that you are in charge. The worst punishment you can get in life is to feel that 'it is all up to me'. That is a very sad and lonely place. Graveyards are full of so-called 'indispensable people'.

THE UNFOLDING

Participate as presence in the unfolding of
Life, this beautiful never repeated moment.
Resting in your unchanging being
Let the gestures of your energy liberate others
Without building solidifying bridges of concept.
Letting go of the delusion of enduring essences
See how each moment arises fresh from nothing.
Bright gift of effulgence, sheen of the open source.

DEVOTION

When we develop devotion, we are small and we are big. We are small because we feel full of respect and faith and can become childlike, undefended and open, and we are big because we feel reassured and can trust that our lives are going in the right way. Our energy can relax and open to embrace what is occurring.

When you have devotion to the dharma the heart opens. Then you see with the eye of the heart, and the eye of the heart sees in ways that ego consciousness cannot. It is for this reason that devotion is very important. Devotion is not an outer practice for those without understanding. It is the highest practice of yogis.

It's not that you either have faith or you don't have faith. It's that faith arises from causes and if we find that the flame of faith is going down we can attend to the causes of this and feed our faith. We are the ones who can direct our own inspiration. We are not puppets dependent on distant forces. The deities will always respond, that is not in doubt. The question is whether we bother to evoke them.

Devotion dissolves reification and it dissolves the solidification that arises from believing in entities. Belief in entities is dissolved by trust in emptiness. Belief in emptiness will dissolve belief in substance. The emptiness of the mind and the emptiness of appearance arise together as sky to sky. Rainbows don't block the sky, they express or display its creativity. When we see that we and all that we encounter are empty of self-substance our isolation dissolves and we are revealed as unfolding radiant display.

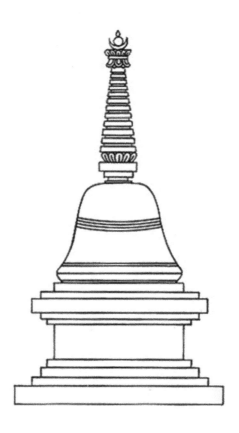

EMPTINESS

RELAX AND RELEASE

Whether the mind is busy
Or quiet,
Relax fixation on what arises
Be aware of your own existence unfolding and vanishing.
Who is the one having this experience?

Our mind,
The basis of our existence,
Is not a thing we can grasp.
How strange, how unexpected.
In our awareness
All things arise:
The sun and the moon arise,
Our bodies arise,
Our thoughts and feelings arise.
If we think of something that is
Not in our awareness
Well, it is now!

If all things arise from the mind itself,
And it is not a thing,
How could no-thing give rise to some-thing?
There are no some-things.

Relax and open
Discover all you have hidden from yourself.

Emptiness is present everywhere. Everything in all circumstances is inseparable from emptiness. These statements are true, and yet emptiness is ungraspable and words cannot encompass it for it lies on the very edge of language. When we speak we create partial truths, little gestures or hints which indicate that at this moment what I say is the view from 'here', the ever-changing site of my unfolding life. We all act as if our words can constitute the whole story, that life can be summed up. In this way we find ourselves in a kind of theatre, the theatre of 'as if', of make-believe. Theatre begins with the suspending of disbelief. When we go to the theatre we know that, on one level, the people who appear on the stage are actors and are paid money to pretend to be somebody else. However when they come on to the stage we are happy to believe that they are the characters whom they present themselves as being. We want to be taken in. We want to get lost in make-believe. This is very profound. It illuminates the ego's desire to merge with the object, to get rid of the burden of lonely isolation. The relief of seeing this, however, is short-lived. Being a worldly person and being a spiritual person are both delusions if we are not present to and as the ground of being. Merely changing the shape and colour of our delusions will not bring awakening. But seeing the delusion as an illusion reveals the non-duality of form and emptiness.

All buddhist cultures seem to have developed a deep aesthetic sensibility. As reliance on conceptualisation falls away, beauty becomes very important. For example, if you go walking in Himalayan valleys, you will see lots of little stupas exquisitely placed in the environment. One might imagine that Cézanne had been wandering there to study composition for the stupas are so perfectly placed. Opening to emptiness dissolves our learned artifice letting intuitive spontaneity shape our activity.

In the beginning our practice requires conscious motivation and intentional effort. As we become more at home in the practice and see it as an integral part of our lives, we find ourselves more integrated in our world. We find ourselves speaking and behaving in ways that 'fit' the situation. Emptiness is seeping through every aspect of our lives and dissolving the seeming solidity of concepts. Effortless co-emergence, the play of emptiness, becomes how we are. Emptiness shows life as simple and precise. Opening to this intuitive spontaneity is the end of striving.

Samsara is a network of concepts and ideas which we seem to find infinitely seductive. Some of these thoughts may appear to be very important. Important or not, however, thoughts are always empty. When we were translating our texts in India, CR Lama always ended his foreword with the words, *"If there is any merit in this book, we offer it to all beings. If there is no merit in this, we put it back into emptiness."* Either way it doesn't make any difference. We just do what we do and having done it, something else will happen. The key thing here is to practise activity without investment, without hope of a return. We give each moment precisely what is required for that moment. We don't try to make a profit. We don't try to fill a doggie bag that will carry over into the next moment. Just this, then this, then this... Each moment is sufficient unto itself.

Here we are in this flow of experience, so what is the source of the flow? It is the wellspring of the dharmadhatu, emptiness itself. Emptiness is flowing out of emptiness, through emptiness, into emptiness.

SPECIAL

DON'T TRY TOO HARD

Be with yourself with unwavering attention.
What is called 'yourself' is both experience and experiencer.
Let the experience show you where the experiencer is.
Being on that point, the door opens
Step through your fleeting experience into awareness itself.
With alert yet passive receptive presence
Be exquisitely with whatever is occurring.
Thoughts, feelings and sensations easily pull our attention
This way and that.
Again and again relax and release your engagement.
All that arises goes free by itself.
Who is the one who remains when its children die?
Your naked self is fine as it is and needs no covering.
If you try to catch it, it will always vanish
For you are not who you think you are.
Your true being is not like anything else.
It doesn't fit any concept or category.
It is not familiar and yet is closer to you than your breath.
Actively look for it and you will always find something else.

Of course in terms of practice it helps to believe that the teachings we follow are very special and very precious. Then we will treat them with respect and try to use them well. Yet the function of the teaching is to help us to awaken to the unborn empty actuality, how we actually are and how appearances actually are. Awakening to emptiness we find all is as it is, with no division of special and ordinary.

This whole world is the same river with each of us a little ripple within it. However, when we sit in ego isolation within the bubble of ourselves, we protect our difference from other people because we want to be unique and special. Actually we are made out of the same stuff as everyone else. This does not mean that we are the same as other people. We are neither the same nor different; we are each unique forms which are inseparable from the open empty dharmadhatu.

One source, one mother

Naked dancer, free of cover

Cut my root and set me free

Labdron mother, dance with me!

CUT THE CRAP

THE SETTING

The way is lost
The forest deep
Too scared to move
Too scared to sleep

Aroused, confused
The passions swirl
Mind and world
The banshees skirl.

Turbulent terror
Invents fearsome night.
Each unknown sound
Explodes as fright.

I'm caught, I'm caught
By predatory thoughts
They tear me apart and
Devour my own heart
Feeding on me
Feeding on me.

I hate them
Yet I call them.
My sense of me and mine
Calls them here to dine.

The more they get
The more they want
The more they take
The more they taunt.

They love the real, the substantial
They yearn for solid food
And it's my own stupid attachment
Creates the essence they find so good.

Feed them I must, I just have to
But I can feed them in fear or in joy
As long as I'm steeped in delusion
I'm in fear as their helpless toy.

Yet seeing that I am illusion
As is everything else that I see
I can give them my own dear body.
By this gift I'll set us all free.

Here in this happy cemetery
Vultures feed on the dead
When life leaves the body
It's loathed and dumped far from its bed.

The body as thing has no value
It's my attachment that makes it so fine
As investment in this site of identity fades
The corpse rots as pus and slime.

 If the ego does not die
The mind itself will never fly
So dissolve attachment
In the limitless sky.

INTENTION

The cemetery has come to where I stay
And demons visit me each day
Yet I won't trouble to chase them away
It's just my mind at play
It's just my mind at play
Cut!

Doubts and fears are everywhere
Each being I meet is full of care
Depressed, anxious, too much to bear
All hopes sucked into the demon's lair.
Cut!

What seems to be given is not the case
Illusion, confusion has us in their tight embrace
Stop running and turn, meet them face to face
I make my stand in infinite space.
Cut!

CUTTING AWARENESS FREE OF EGO'S DREAM

Cut off ego by dissolving its home
Cut ignorance and rest in mind alone
Cut identification with this body, soon to be dead
Cut up the corpse-like finite, sever the head
Cut through to the source, mince the brain

Cut down assumptions, dead flesh feels no pain
Cut out activity, grinding muscles, tendons and bones
Cut reification, slicing heart, liver and all vital zones
Cut self-concern, no essence in ego
Cut by not cutting, be space and let go

REFUGE

Taking refuge in my thoughts, I'm lost.
Cutting that false refuge I'm tossed aloft
Into the space where I always have been
Awakening to what is, as if from a dream

Trusting the buddha, I give up the fight
Trusting the dharma, all will be right
Trusting the sangha, I know I belong
With these as my refuge I'm fearless and strong
Relaxed and at ease watch phenomena flow
Whatever comes comes, whatever goes goes

BODHICITTA

I like myself, I like me a lot
Though in snares of self-criticism I often am caught
Yet what of the others – who're a lot like me.
Can I be happy if they are not free?

Each sentient being feels themselves to be
Someone apart, trapped in autonomy.
To unfold their tight enfolded fold
I will cut the root of all they hold.
Nothing to grasp at and no need to cling
The sweet song of freedom is all that we'll sing.

Cut off the old stuff you take to be you.
Cut to the chase, seek the fresh that rings true.
Cut loose into welcoming space, there's nothing to do.
Cut the crap, be yourself, the heart light shines through.

Cut free of the past for it's long gone.
Cut free of the future that strings you along.
Cut free of the present, no territory to control.
Cut free in this moment and let life unfold.

PURIFICATION

Unchanging sweet being you're never defiled
For nothing can touch you, dear innocent child.
Yet I'm caught in confusion and feel that I'm bad
Identifying with failure and sad times I've had.

Please send me your blessing.
Let it flow from your heart.
Then I'll fill myself with it
Till old habits depart.

So now I am pure
All delusion is gone
My mind is vast space
Filled with radiant dawn.

GURU YOGA

You teach me, you reach me
You show me a way
Though I have to refind it
Many times each day.

You're all that I need
And you're not far away
I find me in you
Through merging in play.

VIEW

Poor little self you're so lonely.
No wonder you're troubled and sad.
Can't you see that you're trapped in a bubble
Caught by thoughts that are driving you mad?

Yet these thoughts are actually fleeting.
They have no true substance at all.
Your prison is just an illusion
What stops you from walking through walls?

The felt knowledge that proves you are you
Is delusion, seclusion, quite untrue.
Habitual belief leads to more repetition
Confirming each construct as your true condition.

It's your own work that maintains the illusion,
You seek comfort but find only confusion.
Your work is in vain and brings only pain
For constructs are fragile and do not remain.

So let go of effort and see what occurs
When you just do nothing at all.
Relax, be at ease in mere presence
Life tumbles as freely as water falls.

As 'I', 'me', 'myself' lose their power to control
You'll be healed by sweet mother space.
Open and clear with no basis for fear
Effortless radiance displays her true face.

As the cocoon falls away your effort will cease
For the ease that you sought is revealed.
Then you'll see with surprise, through your bright shining eyes
That it's your own thoughts that had you concealed.

SAVOUR THE FLAVOUR

Attracting builders and vultures
Each richly flavoured thought
Although seemingly something
Is actually naught.

On its way out, and
Ready to vanish
It can't be caught and
Need not be banished.

Yet gathering thoughts
Seek to build on my form
Their energy feeding
The myth that it's born.

Then come the vultures
Who know that it's dead
Their critical beaks
Tear the limbs from the head.

The flavours of thoughts
Are diverse and beguiling
These savours of emptiness
Indicate substance worth finding.

Yet again and again
The dream of essence deludes
As thoughts rich and empty
Neither start nor conclude.

More like a perfume
Than a piece of thick steak
Pervading the air
Over each empty plate.

CUTTING

Cut the body cut the thought
Cut the feeling cut the talk
Cut cut cut all you have got.

Cut your family cut your name
Cut your history cut your fame
Cut cut cut fear of going insane.

Cut the future cut the past
Cut the changes cut what lasts
Cut cut cut free the mind so vast.

Cut the hope cut the fear
Cut those far cut those near
Cut cut cut in the space so clear.

Cut on self cut on other
Cut on father cut on mother
Cut cut cut all you use for cover.

Cut the grass
Cut your spending
Cut your needs
They're never ending.

Cut consumption
Become thinner
Cut your rest and
Be a winner.

Cutting down and
Cutting back –
When nothing's left
You'll feel the lack.
Cut cut cut

Cutting pleasure
Cutting pain
Cutting feeling –
Where's the gain?

If you cut
To seize control
You'll have to cut
Life's every roll.

Cut the leaves and
Cut the branch
Yet cutting gives
New growth a chance.
Cut cut cut

So stop blind cutting
Let life flow free
Just cut the root
Of samsara's tree.

Let go of object
Cut subject too
Cut all that binds
Cut me, cut you.

Cut attachment
Cut hope and fear
Cut through to space
Where all is clear.
Cut cut cut

Merged in space
I'm not a thing
No form to catch
No bell to ring.

Open and empty
Yet still right here
Presence of nothing
Quite free of fear.

Mind without limits
Unconditioned, undefined
This ground of experience
To difference is blind.
Cut cut cut

Indivisible space
Is the infinite field
Within which I move
And to which I yield.

Without propositions
There's no basis for fear
Self-doubt and anxiety
Can never come near.

In cutting the entity
Free by the root
We collapse all support
For anxiety's hook.
Cut cut cut

Worries about money
Ageing and death
Fears that my wishes
Will never be met

Anxiety over what
The future will bring
Agitation, perturbation
And life's painful sting

Doubts and preoccupations
Hover in my head
Despair and desolation
Make my heart their bed.
Cut cut cut

Relax and rest easy
These moments will pass
By being here with them
They're gone really fast.

Not blocking what happens
Just relinquish control.
Take early retirement
From vigilance patrol.

With heart open wide
I impose no division.
This healing whole
Accepts ego's submission.
Cut cut cut

Nothing to fear and
Nothing to hide
At home in the city
And the wild countryside.

The clarity of presence
Shows the first hint of danger
Attachment breeds delusion –
Fear this, not the stranger.

By cutting attachments
And ignorance too
Though problems remain
They don't get through.

Space is wide open and
I'm bright and clear
Participation is easy
When you're free of fear.
Cut cut cut

OFFERING

All sites of delusion, now less than dust
This empty illusion offered to those we trust
Buddhas, awakened ones, please accept this as light
And with your compassion dispel our dark night.
Then for all who rely on an object for joy
Let this light appear as houses, food and toys
And for those who are weak, cast down and abused
Let this light appear as protection and all that reassures.

DEDICATION

Cut free of the deed and all merit too.
I didn't do this for me nor was it for you
For self and other, they do not exist
Mere phantoms, illusions, dispelling like mist.
All beings are radiance, the display of the source
So we let go of effort and let life take its course.

HOSPITALITY

In the Sanskrit term 'dharmadhatu', 'dharma' refers to phenomena and 'dhatu' indicates 'space', thus it refers to the space within which all phenomena arise. I have recently started translating it as 'infinite hospitality' because the space of the mind can be hospitable to anything, just as the mirror is hospitable to whatever image arises within it.

Pure presence, in having no defining content of its own, is invulnerable. On the level of openness there is no need to edit our experience. In meditation we relax into this open presence and let go of our habits of judging occurrences in terms of good and bad. Non-dual wisdom offers hospitality to everything. If we have a stream of negative thoughts we welcome them. They are just thoughts. They are not going to harm our mind which is open and free of self-substance. They are transient illusory forms that fill the space of awareness and then vanish. If they are allowed to come and go, and if we remain relaxed and open, then they leave no trace, just as reflections leave no trace in the mirror. It is our limited and limiting ego-formation which is selective and self-protective. As the habitual patterns which maintain this illusory formation are let go of, we have a more precise sense of all the aspects of the emergent field and so our responses are more fitting. This is the basis of non-reificatory compassion.

Now is whenever 'now' is. 'Here' is wherever 'here' is. 'I' am whoever 'I' am here and now. The mirror is showing whatever it's showing because of its hospitality. We manifest as selfish, stupid and blind when we don't recognise and honour the hospitality of the here and now. We can integrate anything into the practice. Don't block whatever is occurring, don't enter into judgement about it. Just offer hospitality to it. The nature of the mind is infinite hospitality. It is always open, always welcoming.

The more we privilege relaxation over arousal the more the felt sense of openness becomes our home base. The more we experience our own being as empty, the more generous and welcoming we can be to whatever is arising. This is the basis of unlimited hospitality. We see that there is nothing in the object which can harm us and nothing in ourselves which can be damaged. Moreover we see that there is nothing in the object to benefit us and nothing in ourselves which can be benefitted. The truth of this is revealed when we let go of identification with the deluding fantasy of the ego as an enduring knowable entity.

HAPPY BIRTHDAY

FIRST BIRTH

Welcomed at birth
by my karma
I forgot who I was

Welcomed at birth
by concepts I never
forgot my conditioning

Welcomed at birth
by my parents I never
forgot my alienation

SECOND BIRTH

Welcomed at birth
by the Buddha I never
forgot my refuge

Welcomed at birth
by the Dharma I never
forgot the transmission

Welcomed at birth
by the Sangha I never
forgot my place

THIRD BIRTH

Welcomed at birth
by my Guru I never
forgot my new family

Welcomed at birth
by my Yidam I never
forgot my samaya

Welcomed at birth
by Dakinis I never
forgot how to dance

FOURTH BIRTH

Welcomed at birth
by my own source I never
forgot my integrity

IMPERMANENCE

TAKE IT EASY

Everything is impermanent, vanishing by itself
So don't hold onto appearances as if they were reliable.
Don't try to retain what you think you know and like
Don't push events away because they seem too much
For these involvements mean this busy work of ego will never end.
There will always be something to be done, to be improved or avoided
So just stay present with the one who does the doing.

Release identification and rest in your mind as it is.
Like the mirror, remain
Relaxed, open and present
Then you will see
Your own busyness
Still striving to obscure
What you had been looking for.

The most basic and central of all the Buddha's teachings – the one that you find in all the buddhist schools – is the fact of impermanence. Another way of expressing this is to say that all experience is dynamic. By simply staying open and relaxed we start to experience directly the effortless coming and going of all phenomena. Everything I call 'I, me, myself', and everything about which I say such things as, *'This is another person,' 'This is a house,' 'This is a town,'* are aspects of change. They are examples of how change patterns itself; they express the autopoiesis of change. These identifications only appear to be discrete and enduring entities because we construe them in that way. All appearance, all experience, whether it seems to be the 'subject' or the 'object' is in fact the actuality of change. The one thing which doesn't change never appears as some thing. It is awareness inseparable from space. Our ungraspable presence is the one true refuge, a refuge we will never find yet will always be.

The Buddha's teaching on impermanence points to the fact of the ungraspability of experience. Embracing this can help us relax and accept that flow is what there is. If we can trust the flow of life, if we can allow ourselves to be flowing with others in the flow, then we will find that what we need situationally comes to hand, comes to mind.

Since all phenomena are impermanent they will go by themselves, so there is no need for us to push them away. Since all phenomena are impermanent they will go by themselves, so neither is there any point in trying to hang onto them. This is the essence of the dzogchen practice.

The Buddha's teachings are radical, rooted in open spaciousness. They are disturbing, turning our world upside-down and shifting the basis of who we think we are. Everything that we know, everything that we're connected with, still appears but we start to see it differently. If we focus on the difference we will feel disturbed, and this disturbance opens some cracks in our sealed and limited view of what is going on. These cracks let in warm fresh air which gradually melts the ice-palace of our delusion and frees us back into the flow. Reflecting on impermanence is an important preparatory practice since the more we see that impermanence is the actual state of affairs, the more we see that relying on phenomena to provide a true refuge is not wise.

Contemplation of impermanence functions like a screwdriver, gradually loosening the screws that fix your beliefs and assumptions in place. A good practice is like a good friend, one who reveals more and more qualities and more and more richness the longer you know them.

IMPERMANENCE

Recollection of impermanence is the simple heart of practice.
Impermanence shows us emptiness.
Impermanence shows us the source of our mind.
Impermanence offers us the courage to fully live our life
With all its strangeness and disappointment.

Impermanence is very sweet and precious.
Impermanence opens the way to live in the moment
Showing us there is nowhere else to live.
The wonderful fact of impermanence is freely available
Everywhere! Beautiful!

Impermanence is everywhere, all the time,
In everything you do:
Parking your car, going to work,
Going to the toilet, doing the dishes.
Everything which appears, disappears.
You breathe out
And suddenly you are breathing in.
All appearance is the flow of change.
Nothing to grasp yet
Everything to savour in its perfect moment.

Mirror

Infinite heart

The infinity of the heart
Is peaceful and unchanging,
Open and empty like a mirror.

A mirror does not change.
When you look in the mirror you see the reflections move.
Reflection, potentiality, creativity, is always changing,
Infinitely showing its empty self-formations,
The gift of our unchanging mind.

Our openness,
Our emptiness,
Our ungraspability
Is the empty stage, the space of revelation.

SIMPLE PURITY

From the very beginning the mind has been completely pure.
There is no fault, no error, no taint.
The mind that is described as being like this
Is our own mind,
It is the mind that we already are.
From the very beginning our basic presence
Has supported us in everything.

Any faults,
Any flaws,
Any errors made are momentary
Contingent movements on the level of reflection.
The reflection does not destroy the mirror.
The reflection of something ugly doesn't make the mirror break.
The reflection of something beautiful doesn't cause the mirror to smile.
The mirror is always open without fear or favour to whatever is arising.
The mirror is the best host:
Never judging her guests
They are free to be
Just how they are.

Whatever faults,
Whatever mistakes,
Whatever errors you have ever made,
Have not fundamentally contaminated you
Have not distorted you.
Have not imprisoned you.
Events and patterns come and go
Revealed by our pure being
The source of infinite light.
Hello, Buddha.

Buddhism considers the mind not as a container which can be filled, but as a clarity which reveals. The traditional example used to illustrate this is the mirror and its reflections. The more we see how all phenomena are arising and passing, we can see that the immediacy of presentation and the immediacy of self-liberation are simultaneous. The open emptiness of the mirror is inseparable from the rich appearance of complex reflections.

If you go to a hairdresser they will hold a mirror behind your head. When you look in the mirror in front of you, you see the reflection of the mirror behind you and in that way you can see how they have cut your hair at the back. Without the mirror you couldn't see that. A mirror helps you to see things you couldn't see otherwise. The teaching and the teacher in the state of transmission is like a mirror and by looking in this moment we can see something more of ourselves. It's not that the teacher is teaching you about yourself, but rather the clarity of the situation lets you see yourself as you actually are and not as you think you are.

If you hold a mirror in your hand and move it around, it will show many different impressions. As you turn it, it will be open to whatever is in front of it. It doesn't accumulate images; rather it reveals them and then releases them. Reveals and releases... Because something has already been shown in the mirror that does not mean something similar cannot be shown again. Each time a reflection is revealed, it has the immediacy of its direct showing; it becomes present to us.

Dust will form on a mirror. When we talk of the mind as being like a mirror this is only a simile. The space-like unborn being of the mind offers no basis or surface for dust to adhere to. This presents the question, when you sit in meditation and a thought seems to stick to you, what is it sticking to? When the mind's unchanging openness is obscured what is it obscured by? How does the unsubstantial appear substantial to us? These questions will take us deeper into the practice if we stay with direct enquiry free of conceptual elaboration.

We say the mind is like a mirror and that it is the emptiness of the mirror that allows everything to be revealed. 'I, me, myself' is like the doppelgänger of the mirror. It's like the mirror's public relations department. Instead of just being relaxed and fully present moment by moment, it feels the need to issue a press release: *"This is to announce, I am happy!"* All day long these little statements are being issued. Who is the one who is issuing the statements? This is the empty nature of the mind itself. The ego is the hustling middle-man, creating a function for himself by linking aspects that are always already inseparable.

The mirror seems to be showing me my face but of course it's actually showing me a reflection of my face. My face and its reflection are not the same. It's the same in the meditation. We get caught up in an experience which occurs. What we get caught up in is a reflection and the one who gets caught up is also a reflection. Yet our mind itself is always the mirror and never a reflection.

Infinite mind like a mirror

This mind, our mind, is infinite.
Empty of substance,
Fresh awareness,
Uncovered, unconditioned,
Has not been made and will never end.
Completely empty and yet always full,
Like a mirror showing reflections
Endlessly appearing yet without real existence.
The ground of the reflection
Is the emptiness of the mirror.
If the mirror were not empty
There would be no reflections.
If the mind were not empty
We would not experience countless appearances
Every moment forever.

Welcoming Space

When we relax into the presence of our being, there is enough space for everything just as it is. Our open spaciousness is infinite and beyond overwhelm and so we don't need to seek control, anxiously editing what appears in terms of 'good', 'bad', 'for me', 'against me', and so on. Everything that arises occurs within the mirror-like revealing space of awareness, and this mirror does not change. The reflections in a mirror change but the mirror itself does not change. When we see this directly we can relax and allow whatever arises to be there without hope of gain or fear of loss. No reflection can destroy a mirror, no arising can destroy or mark or condition the nature of the mind. Something really horrible, really gross, put in front of a mirror won't crack the mirror. The mind itself is similarly stable and indestructible, vajra. It is open and empty and infinite. It is devoid of substance, has no essence and is never found existing as an entity. This infinite awareness is inseparable from everything that occurs. It is the ground and basis of these appearances which are themselves devoid of substance. Our indestructible awareness offers infinite hospitality to whatever occurs without harm to itself. This is the true refuge that shows that everything is simply as it is, complete and requiring neither addition nor subtraction.

Awareness can integrate everything since everything is inseparable from it. It is the ego aspect of ourselves which becomes tremulous and upset, since the ego, in its limitation, cannot cope with everything. We are both our limited physical existence and our infinite awareness. It is not a matter of having to choose one or the other but of awakening to the integration of our two modes. If this is awakened to, our sense of our physical existence as the expression of our individuality is released and our embodiment becomes what it has always been, an aspect of the play of energy of the non-dual field. Of course if you open to your awareness you can still be hit by a car and die.

If you think, *"I am just this physical form and when I die that is it, so I have to get the most out of this life. I have got to make the best life for myself that I can,"* you are struggling to optimise the finite. But how do you get the most out of life? What is the best thing to do? What will make me happy? How will I know? There are so many options for activity – and yet each is finite, impermanent – a sandcastle on the beach of time. Yet our ever-present awareness is unchanging, infinite and always already here. If we are present with whatever is occurring we will always be where we are, content with life as it is.

The quality of being oneself, open and present, is more important than any interpretation or understanding that can arise, for every understanding is a mere event in time which inevitably vanishes. You may have had the experience in school of writing an essay. You really get into it, you finish it, you hand it in, you get a mark – and life moves on. All the focus and effort that went into the project dissolves. It was just a moment. You fall in love. It is just a moment. You eat a good meal. It is just a moment. Nothing can be grasped. You cannot take it with you, but who is the one who remains after the event? You are still going on. 'Someone' is always here. Who is the one who is always here? Since you were born you have always been 'you'. You haven't been the same size, you haven't been doing the same things, you haven't had the same interests or the same friends but somehow you have always been you. What is that you-ness of you? It is not a narrative or a mystical soul essence. It is our unborn presence of emptiness.

This is the truth of the mind itself. By relaxing into this open moment the various turbulent movements of life – happiness, sadness, closeness and distance – are seen to just come and go. Whatever the circumstances we are here – open, spacious, and infinitely hospitable.

NATURE

It is not that this world is a dreadful place which we need to get out of. Rather it is that this is a wonderful world which we don't quite live in – we don't fully participate in it because we are not fully present. The horrors of the world are the products of our imagination, our plans, expectations and fantasies. These are all driven by the two-stroke engine pulsing between desire and aversion.

In thogal the continuous process of experience is described as 'dorje lug-gu gyud'. Lug-gu means sheep and gyud means a chain. You can often see a line of sheep going one after the other along a little track on the hillside. Sheep follow, follow, follow... Likewise we have thoughts that follow, follow, follow... and they leave tracks. If you recognise that the thought or the image, in the moment that it arises, is nothing at all, then you won't put extra valency on to it, nor will it leave tracks. Appearance is self liberating when left alone. This is why the instruction is always, "Don't enter into judgement!" However you have to hold this lightly as even the most negative thoughts and extreme judgements have no ground other than the dharmadhatu. A judgement arising with duality and that same form of judgement arising in non-duality are not the same, and yet they are.

Saraha said that in the winter water turns to ice and then in the summer the water evaporates. So what then is the true state of water he asked. Sometimes our mind freezes like ice; we become very sharp, we become very definite and we can't move. Sometimes we are relaxed and flowing like water, able to adapt to any shape that is around. Other times we get a bit spaced out and dispersed, like steam or mist. We can be each of these three possibilities. It is important to be able to become like ice, to take on a definite shape. It is important to be able to become like steam, to be diffuse and pervasive. It is important to be able to flow, like a river. Problems arise when we adopt a mode that is at odds with circumstances, for then we are out of balance with our environment. Our practice is to develop the freedom to move through the various possibilities of our existence in keeping with the experiential field as it arises.

We can be like seaweed swaying in the tides, sliding over other people, close enough to touch yet not scratching, forcing or demanding. By being moved myself, I am part of the co-emergent movement along with you. By not fixing the definition of my identity in a particular pattern of movement, I don't mind being affected by you. All my shapes are me, equally me. I, as open awareness, gain or lose nothing by shifting shape. Allowing my shaping to be co-emergent, my energy is for the other, for the world, for spontaneous intrinsically ethical participation in the field of non-duality. As we awaken to our groundless ground we find the free movement of its energy arises effortlessly.

Allowing the mind to be as it is, to unfold as it will without interference, is referred to as 'rang bab' in Tibetan which means 'falling by itself', as a waterfall does. A waterfall falls by itself in relation to rocks and wind. Similarly the flow of our mind is just tumbling down, unpredictable, shifting between coherent and incoherent. By allowing that to happen, which is to say not interfering with what is happening, you start to trust, "Oh, life finds its own way." In particular, you see that, "I don't need to be in charge."

I was watching a video for children about an elephant who wanted to fly. The elephant couldn't fly, but some friends managed to get him up a tree, and then a friendly cloud came and floated underneath. The elephant jumped from the tree onto the cloud and he fell right through it. In the same way, emptiness is like a cloud and we are like elephants. Until we become very light, light and empty, we will keep falling through. We won't be able to stay in emptiness until we are empty too.

All the experiences of our lives are like birds flying in the sky. Maybe you go out for a walk and suddenly a memory comes into your mind. This is a beautiful bird. It has flown into your mind and then it flies out. However, birds can also shit on your head. If you get caught up in a thought it can start to grind. Something else is happening then. This beautiful little humming-bird was followed by an eagle and then a vulture. Yet, they too will fly away. Everything flies away. Only the sky remains.

There are choices to be made. We can be a hunter, or a bird, or we can be like the sky. When we are like the sky everything will come to us and everything will go – we can enjoy the birds as they fly. Or we can be a hunter, always trying to catch or kill the birds. This creates a constant arousal in our mind as we are always on the lookout, always ready to pounce. A grasping attitude like that blinds us to the beauty and freedom of the situation. However, if we become a bird we will find that the hunter will come and get us and then we will sing our life away in a little box.

When we see that through our identification with our thoughts we are like a bird, it is not helpful to dream of escaping to a land without hunters. For as long as there are birds there will be hunters. However even inside our cage, even if it is very small, there is still some space. By integrating with that space the freedom of our life is revealed even though our circumstances are very constrained. That is why in our practice we aim to integrate with space as quickly and easily as we can. It is through resting in space as space that we see that the bird and the hunter have the same nature; they are both thoughts, both identifications devoid of inherent self-identity.

As long as the seed is just a seed on its own, its potential is latent. Whether it might grow into a flower or a weed does not matter too much. Weeds only become problematic if sprouting occurs in a place where you do not want them. While sitting in meditation our thoughts, be they good or bad, do not lead to activity in the world and so are not very dangerous. This allows us to get close to them, without either encouraging or blocking, and to see what they actually are. This encourages the ripening of wisdom. Of course our practice, in making us more sensitive and attentive, can also make us more aware of difficulties and suffering in the world around us. Due to this it can appear to be increasing our own suffering. However if we stay with what is occurring and allow ourselves to be touched and moved, this will encourage the ripening of compassion.

This evening I noticed a woman out in the garden watering the flowers. But of course she wasn't just watering the flowers, she was watering the weeds as well because the flowers and the weeds go together. If you want the flowers to grow, you bring water and nutrition for the soil, and this makes it a very nice place for weeds to grow as well. It is exactly the same in spiritual development: the more you nourish your potential the more you become aware that new kinds of weeds are starting to sprout.

We are like children who spend the morning building a sandcastle on the edge of the sea and then come back from lunch and are very unhappy because the sea has washed our castle away. Everything we do is only sand castles. It is an absolute fantasy to imagine that our life's work is more than that. That doesn't mean we shouldn't build sandcastles, for our physical presence in the world predisposes us to engaged activity. The key point is to see that all we do and all that happens to us is like a dream, a mirage, an illusion. Appearance is undeniable yet is empty of substance. There is nothing there to cling on to. When we grasp at objects we are actually grasping at our own conceptual constructs.

The waves of objects coming towards us, and the waves of our projections going out towards them, interact ceaselessly. There is always something new to be interested in and to respond to. When waves meet in the sea their turbulence generates white froth. Similarly we pass our lives in the evanescent frothy bubble of each encapsulating, over-invested moment.

If you go out on a boat and the wind is blowing, you can watch the waves moving. Along comes a seagull, and lands on the water. It had been flying and now it's bobbing on the waves. It's having a little rest, but what it's sitting on is moving. Our mind is like this. Moments in time flow on like waves in the sea. Each wave discloses a thought that seems interesting and the seagull of our attention lands on it, believing it to be the site of nourishing fish. However, in the very moment that you think *"This is where I belong,"* you are being moved along. All manifestation is dynamic, and our attempts to stabilise movements distract us from the opportunity to be present as our mind itself, the one aspect of life that is still.

In the fairy-tale of Sleeping Beauty, after she pricks her finger on her birthday, she falls into a deep sleep. Gradually the wild plants, the briars and brambles grow over her. But one day a young prince sets out to find the princess. He enters the dark forest and approaches the mass of sharp thorns. Drawing his sword he cuts his way through it until he finds her. Then with one tender and gentle kiss, he awakens the maiden. Many people see spiritual life as being like this. They imagine all beings to be Sleeping Buddhas, overgrown by different kinds of conditioning and karma. And so, in heroic mode, they vow to draw the holy sword of truth, cut through the obstacles and liberate them. This is a fairy-tale too. Actually we each have to learn to work with circumstances and find the way to see that obstacles themselves are the path and there is no hidden treasure elsewhere. The place to find the treasure is always exactly where we are.

In autumn the squirrels come to the end of their busy period. They are collecting the last nuts before winter. They hide the nuts sometimes under the ground, sometimes in little holes in trees. Unfortunately the memory of the squirrel is not so good which is why you often see them in the early spring time scrabbling around here and there, digging in the earth, trying to find where they buried their nuts. In the same way, we store bits of our lives, our values and identities, in different places and people. As these others become significant for us it is as if part of us is embedded in them and can only be experienced by us by our being with them. We seem to have found a reliable way to bring the past into the future, storing up treasures for later when we will need them. But objects change, people change, our moods and desires change. And when we visit places, people, ideas and so on that were once so important for us, we may find they have become mere echoes. The past is gone, the future is unknowable. All we have is the chance to open and be fully present now. It is more useful to follow the Buddha's example than to try to be a successful squirrel.

In the springtime in the country you can see small lambs jumping about. The field is wide and they bounce about and run around. Their delightful energy is non-productive. It is the pure joy and simple enthusiasm of being alive. If we feel more like a tired old sheep who has seen it all before then we need to actually taste the fresh experience of the field. We are tired because we are burdened by responsibilities and our concepts are tired, over-used, worn out. But if we can put them aside and be with what is – well then, lovely! The infinite spacious field of the dharmadhatu is ever-fresh and radiant with unpredictable display. Meditation lets us slip off our tedious assumptions and frolic in the boundless space of the mind. It is not so serious.

When we say that something is good and another thing is bad, we bring some aspects of the world forward and push others into the background. Selective attention, habitual interpretation and biased judgement fill our own plate with a very narrow selection from the infinite buffet of the world. In this regard we are like a gardener toiling to make the world the way they would like it to be. Yet if we walk out on the wild mountains we see all kinds of plants and bushes growing freely and they are fine just as they are. The ego, in cultivating a personal garden, is ignoring the generous bounty of nature.

NOURISHMENT

Tibetans have a word 'cha' which means 'a share', or 'a portion'. It indicates what our slice is. Our slice of the world is revealed to us through our participation. We get what we get, and working with what we get keeps us alive and connected with what is vital. Imagining that we should be getting something else, something even better, means that we don't see what is on our own plate. To be always looking at somebody else's plate is not very useful.

The purpose of eating is to satisfy the sensation of taste in the mouth and the sensation of hunger in the stomach thereby ensuring that we take in enough nourishment to sustain body and mind. The purpose of meditation is similar. First of all, it has to please our mouth: we have to actually enjoy doing the meditation. For myself, I don't like broccoli. I avoid eating it, so there would not be much point in me praying to the Broccoli Buddha. It is important to find a practice that tastes sweet on our tongue and gives us increasing clarity. It is not enough to do it just because somebody told us to. We need to check into our own experience, our own sensation. 'How is this affecting me?' Buddhism is pragmatic in orientation, the methods being designed to give specific results. We don't do practice for the sake of just doing something to pass the time. Our practice is grounded in our intention and this intention needs to be heartfelt if it is going to be sustained.

If you have a cup and pour water into it, it will fill up. Even something as big as a football stadium will fill up once a hundred thousand people are inside. Think of all the experiences you have had today. How come you are not filled up? Sometimes we do feel overwhelmed and all we want is for people to back off. We seem to have reached the limit of our capacity. This is because our mind's surface has become sticky and events then become agglutinative. We are filled up with sticky rice. It all feels too much. But if the next moment we are offered an experience we find pleasurable we take a big bite. We have suddenly found some more space. The mind's nature is space, it is ego's involvement that limits our capacity to be available. Relax and release. All arisings are self-liberating in the infinity of awareness.

In our lives we each build up, layer by layer, a great lasagne of meaning, and as we know, lasagne is very heavy. A great deal of our suffering arises because our experience of ourselves and our environment is mediated through our habitual stories. These stories have a tilt or bias and this generates a selectivity in our attention which blocks many of the other possibilities that we might entertain. The purpose of meditation is to put our assumptions into question so that narrative can be connective and communicative rather than self-reflexively reassuring to our anxious ego.

The tradition has general guidelines on when to use each of the practices, and we have to remember that each of these practices is a method. Methods are situationally, rather than intrinsically, valid. Take potato peelers, for example. Their function is to remove potato skin and they do that very well. I enjoy peeling potatoes but if I have beautiful small, new potatoes I wouldn't want to peel them. No matter how efficient my potato peeler is, it is unhelpful in relation to new potatoes. The Tibetan tradition has many different 'potato peelers'. The question is, *'What kind of potatoes is life giving us at the moment?'*

If you are used to eating food with a lot of garlic, salt and chilli, but for some reason you have to eat plain white rice and steamed vegetables, the food will not seem very tasty. You will be yearning for the stimulus that comes from the intense flavours of garlic, salt and chilli. This is our situation. We are addicted to conceptualisation and when somebody has an addiction, whether it's tobacco or alcohol or to any kind of activity, they find themselves returning to that activity because it seems to provide something important. We go back to the familiar because it generates a sense of belonging and competence and pleasurable familiarity. This is why meditation has to be done again and again. We are in the process of getting used to what is actually here. This fresh flavour of the moment may seem bland and boring when we are used to the spices of anxiety, fear, hope, excitement and so on. These tasty supplements are produced by our own mind. When we chase our thoughts and emotions we over-stimulate our palate and then the simple taste of life-as-it-is eludes us. Through practice we relax and come to see that less is more.

When I was a child if I did not eat what was on my plate, the meat and the vegetables, I would not get the dessert. Working with energy is the dessert. First you have to digest the main course, which is awakening to our intrinsic openness. If you only eat pudding all the time your teeth will fall out and you will get a lot of pimples.

In order for the new experience to come, the old experience has to go. Otherwise the new experience would be mixed up with the old experience and the resulting mélange would be neither old nor new. If you go to a restaurant for lunch, if when they bring your food, you notice that the edge of the plate has old dried food on it, you would not be pleased. You might even say to the waiter, *"I'm not happy about this. I want a clean plate for my fresh food."* In the same way when your mind is open, available and free of the past you can enjoy the fresh food of the present moment. However, if the plate of your existence is piled up with an accumulation of old experiences, this will contaminate whatever happens now and the sad mix will not refresh your jaded palate.

The complex is actually simple because our direct experience is of discreet moments, this, this, this. We build complexity by linking one simple moment to another and another and another as thought follows thought. This linking across time creates a sense of density, of solidity, of complexity—so that each moment feels more like a multi-layered club sandwich. This seeming complexity is produced by our mental activity, our conceptual elaboration. By relaxing our own habitual effort each moment is a simple non-fattening snack.

Infinite mind

The mind is infinite.
Something which is infinite has no limits.
If it has no limit it has no edge, no border.
There is nothing outside the mind.
Nothing to export or import.
If it arises for you, it is yours!
So…
Where does it come from?
The mind comes from nowhere
Yet everything comes from the mind.
Finding that is finding yourself.
Yet, sweet and bitter paradox,
It cannot be found.

SAMSARA

Samsara is the attempt to stabilise that which can never be stabilised and so there is no end to it. While we are struggling to do the impossible, we are not attending to the one thing which is stable, the door to nirvana.

In relaxed open spaciousness everything arises just as it is, and this hospitality, free of demand, heals the intense nervous agitation which drives the engine of samsara.

Sitting quietly in meditation you can examine the birth of samsara. When the openness of the mind seems to vanish as we get caught up in whatever is arising, the subject is mesmerised by the object and so forgets the common ground of experience and experiencer. So much turbulence is generated without anything actually having been created. Illusion arises when we take the energy of the mind to be solid. This leads us far from where we are without our arriving anywhere else. The open ground is the mother of samsara but delusion is the father.

You can't grasp the moment, but you can be present in it as it is. You can inhabit it directly or indirectly. Directly inhabiting the moment is called nirvana and indirectly inhabiting the moment is called samsara.

It is not that we fell into samsara a long time ago and now we are struggling to get out of it, as if it were some hellish nightmare. Samsara begins and ends each second, each moment. A thought arises, you fall into it and there is samsara. The thought ends and in that very moment, there is space, and if you are present in the space samsara has gone. Then you see that there is no wall between samsara and awakening. They are not fundamentally different.

The suffering of samsara arises because although we somehow know that we are infinite and unchanging, in our effort to establish the stability of what we take to be our identity, we unhelpfully project our longing for unchanging being on to our individual ego-self, an aspect of experience which is in fact always changing.

If you believe that samsara and nirvana are different then it is as if there are two factories. One factory makes samsara and one makes nirvana. In samsara things are very bad while in nirvana things are very good. If we hold onto this view then we need to close down the Samsara Factory and end the production of suffering. When that is achieved there will be continuous production in the Nirvana Factory and all will be very nice and shiny. This is not the view of dzogchen. According to dzogchen there is one ground, one factory, and from it both samsara and nirvana arise without being produced. This is the Dream Factory of illusion where both are merely reflections in the mirror of the mind.

THERAPY AND BUDDHISM

In my experience as a therapist, I have seen that the practice of meditation can help those who are troubled and lost. It can help them to separate out from their habitual sense of being helplessly merged in the flow of experience. Developing calmness and clarity lets us sit on the bank of the river observing the flow without being pulled in to it. With some direction and support we can all learn to be attentive to, yet not involved in, whatever is occurring. This is a huge relief. I am not my symptom nor my diagnosis. I am the one who can start to see what is going on and what I am up to.

Our meditation is based on emptiness, the emptiness of our mind and the emptiness of all phenomena. Awakening to the illusory nature of existence allows us to not take ourselves too seriously. Impermanent experiences arise and pass and so we learn to participate without reification, releasing the limiting seductions of hopes and fears. Working as a therapist, whether having good sessions or bad sessions, positive transference or negative transference, whatever arises is the play of emptiness. Then there is nothing much to say about our work just, *"Oh yes, another busy day."*

Repeated negative thoughts become like a huge old sofa – very heavy to move, and very tempting to sit in. We can collapse into our neurotic beliefs and feel quite at home. Then you see the world from that point of view. Of course a lot of other things are going on simultaneously but you are now seated comfortably facing in your chosen direction. Doing something new doesn't feel quite as interesting as the repetition of the delicious limitation of this neurosis. Oh, Oh!

Nothing lasts forever. When the spring is here, the flowers come out. When autumn comes, the flowers die, and then in winter little is left above ground. When I began work as a therapist, I didn't know very much but it was spring-time and fresh ideas popped up like flowers. After a while the garden of my practice was blooming. But the years go by and now, although I know a lot more, it's almost winter for me and my professional life will soon end. That's life. So many of the things I could do then, I can't do now. It is time to let go. We take our place in the world according to our seasons. When winter comes enthusiasm declines and our mood is more calm. Knowing the fact of loss, knowing how to let go and experience less than we once did — these poignant experiences can deepen our empathy and allow a deeper acceptance of life. So much therapy theory is focussed on the nature of psychological change, as if change won't happen unless we make it happen. Yet reflecting on our own impermanence reminds us that change is the heart of all experience and the power of our agency is not so great. Change occurs in patients when they open to the ever-changing rhythms of life.

In having our story we need to hold in mind the ingredients that have gone into it. This is easy if you are making a salad, because the ingredients put together in a salad can be quite easily identified. If you're baking something in the oven, like lasagne, then it's not so easy because the heat brings about a transformation. The various flavours run together to create a composite taste. The function of the therapist being mindful in the clinical setting is to help the client eat the raw food of direct experience. Every time you cook experience by putting it in the oven of habit and assumption you kill off a lot of its vitamins. Help the client stay close to the freshness of their experience and support them in seeing the processes through which they construct their composite story. Yes, we do need to have our stories if we are going to function in the world, for this world is largely composed of stories, yet we also need to see that each story we tell is just a story, just one version, just one pattern of what we might present. If we get caught in the story and take it to be the truth then we will lose our clarity.

At the end of the therapy the patient, having been freed from the transference, can now see that the therapist is an ordinary person. That dream of the specialness of this particular other is over. However, that doesn't stop the dreaming. Dreams go on. You end the dream of analysis and you might pick up another dream, perhaps the dream of 'buddhism'. Dream follows dream, each one appearing to be real and true. Lucid dreaming, being awake in the dream, offers the chance to participate without solidification or grasping.

The idea of a divided self can be quite shocking since it puts in question our familiar sense that, 'I'm just me'. In fact we are not divided nor are we unitary. We are multiple, we are myriad energetic forms. Our multiplicity sometimes appears coherent and sometimes appears incoherent. Rather than treating our variety as an orchestra requiring scores and a conductor, we might simply allow our diversity to show itself and collaborate respectfully. Our self is dynamic and relational and so every description we give of ourselves is contextually valid and not intrinsically so. To be a balanced person is to be skilled in facilitating group therapy for our own many different aspects.

WISDOM AND COMPASSION

The balance of wisdom and compassion is very important. Wisdom gives you spaciousness, while compassion gives you connection. These two aspects belong together. They spread from the heart like the two wings of a bird.

Compassion is awakening to the actuality of our connection with others. This connectivity is always already here, present even before we're aware of it. Compassion's quality is connectivity.

All the various tantric practices serve to free the knots which exist in our body and which constrain the energy moving through the channels of the body. This frees us up to have more plasticity and more capacity to move within the endless eddying sway of the world. In this view, wisdom is to be relaxed in open presence, in effortless non-duality with the ungraspable ground of being, while compassion is to become whatever is required in the situation. If we know who we actually are, in knowing that we are nothing we have the potential to be everything that is required.

When we see the wide range of our confusions and the confusions of others, if we can release our habitual judgemental stance, we have more chance to develop our sensitivity to others and to ourselves. Our attunement to the complexity of life helps us to see that there is no easy way to sort out ourselves or others. We all have both confusion and the possibility of awakening from it. This is not the same as being 'sorted'. Integrating with emptiness, with unborn awareness, doesn't remove life's problems or make us 'better people'. The space it opens lets patterns be as they are, transient and impactful. Whether judged helpful or harmful, in emptiness they are empty. That is how they are. Opening to emptiness, we develop compassion free of reification. Not making ourselves into an object or an instrument, neither do we make other people into an object or an instrument. To turn people into something that we use for our own agenda, for our own purpose, is the deep way to pervert all the teachings. Wanting to change people before we have seen their empty illusory nature is a sure way to conflict and violence.

E verything is illusion, mere appearance without substantial essence. Wisdom is to see that everything is illusion. Compassion is to act carefully and helpfully with beings who are trapped in illusion arising from the delusion of believing that phenomena are essentially real in themselves.

H ow are wisdom and compassion activated in our own existence? Essentially wisdom has to do with understanding the illusory nature of our existence. That doesn't mean that it's all a fantasy and so nothing matters, for wisdom is inseparable from compassion, and compassion is to feel the immediacy of the link we have to everything and everyone. Compassion is to trust that being relaxed, open and connected allows a finesse of engagement which is both fundamental and ethical.

Helping other people doesn't require a particular bridge between ourselves and others since we are always already in the emergent world which includes self and others. However the world according to our thoughts and beliefs may be a self-referential world occupied only by ourselves. When we seem to live inside ourselves, protected or restricted by a high threshold, our sense of being an autonomous entity is increased. Yet this sense of individual identity is in fact an energetic resonance within a field of energy. That is to say, we are communication and we shift with the field we inhabit. We are nothing but energy responding to energy.

Other beings are our world. They are not an optional add-on. As long as we see other people as separate from ourselves and from each other we will be making effort to join with them or to get further away from them. That effort will condemn us to artificiality. We are all in this together, although what 'this' is cannot be defined and any agreement about it is bound to be misleading. Tasting the fact of co-emergence makes being available for others as normal as breathing.

PRACTICING THE UNITY OF WISDOM AND COMPASSION

View

Our very being, what and how we actually are, is not a 'thing'. It is an openness within which many appearances seem to expand and contract. Good and bad are both the empty play of the mind. Seeing this, we open to all that occurs without hope or fear.

Space is indestructible, beyond conditioning or contamination. Awakening to our own spaciousness we are freed from bias and selectivity, freed from the urge to control others and identify them as friend or foe. With no thoughts of gain or loss we can give light and love and receive darkness and pain. The emptiness of all manifestation is the one truth. The labelling as good or bad, desirable or undesirable, is mere conditioned contingent opinion, the driver of ceaseless reactivity and disturbance.

Practice

As a practice, we imagine that the centre of our being, our heart, is an infinite clear blue sky. Our ground, our basis, is simply infinite space. We imagine rays of rainbow light arising in this clear blue space, spreading out and making connection with all possible kinds of beings in all possible places. Rays of rainbow light, the blessing of emptiness, touch all beings, awakening them to the light which is their own intrisic quality. We then imagine that from those beings, all their limitations, all the ways in which they are turned against themselves and turned against others, arise and return to us in the form of dark shadows, fearful shapes, poison. All this darkness comes towards us, right into the infinite blue sky of our heart, dissolving into it. We open ourselves to receiving all the pain and limitations of all beings. Who is the one who does this? Our awareness, the inseparability of wisdom and compassion. The darkness is not coming into our narrow ego identity but into the infinity of our open heart. We alternate between focussing on the rays of rainbow light going out to all beings and focussing on their difficulties coming to us. If you feel that the suffering coming towards you is too much then simply focus on the rainbow light spreading from your heart.

Function

This is work our ego cannot do. It is not about forcing ourselves to transcend our limits. Heroic struggle will not free us from the delusion of duality. Such struggle merely affirms our notions of high and low, good and bad. The open heart is beyond duality. It is not a position, or a state, or a belief. It does not stand in relation to anything else. The infinite empty mind can offer everything and receive everything because it does not enter into contradiction or conflict. Non-duality is free of this versus that, self versus other. Without this freedom our compassion will quickly find its limit and our ego will cry out, *'What about me!'* This very simple practice is the integration of wisdom and compassion. Compassion is to have no limits or blocks in relation to all other beings and wisdom is to find oneself inseparable from emptiness, the ground of all. Emptiness refers not just to ourselves and our own heart but to all other beings and all that manifests. Emptiness indicates that all appearance is actually insubstantial. Appearance is concrete and precise in its shape and yet is without individual defining essence. Appearance neither exists nor does not exist; its illusory forms are the creativity of the mind. The mind creates everything and everything exists as the experience of the mind. Unborn and unceasing, this is the immediacy of mind beyond conceptualisation.

Ordinarily we are like a container of some kind. For example, our teacup can only hold so much. If you were to take a gallon of water and try to put it into our teacup there would be a huge puddle on the floor. Due to our identification with our habitual thoughts and feelings we take ourselves to be finite and so are limited in capacity like a small cup. We can't hold very much inside us and easily feel invaded and overwhelmed. Or we take ourselves to be infinite without opening to our infinite ground. Then we do too much, offer too much, and get burnt out and collapse.

The purpose of this practice of imagining oneself to be the infinite clear blue sky, is to open up the cup of the self so that it is both space and source, able to give out infinitely and to take in infinitely. How much can we bear? Well, that depends on who we are in this moment. If we are in our contracted frightened aspect we can't bear very much. Yet when we are less anxious and preoccupied we can cope with more. For as long as we identify with our self-referential ego we will have limited capacity to welcome all that occurs. When we are in our relaxed open aspect, however, we don't have to bear anything or struggle to cope because we are not experiencing the world as burdening us. Then anything and everything becomes possible.

In this practice we are changing gear, moving from excluding whatever does not fit our identity, from being narrow, limited, and defended. Releasing ourselves from these identifications composed of thoughts, memories, emotions, we relax into the infinite intrinsic uncreated mind. This mind is itself the source and field of these limiting factors. Seeing this is the key way to release ourselves from their power to limit. This practice is called tonglen in Tibetan: *tong* indicates 'I give what is positive to others' and *len* indicates 'I take what is negative from others'. This is an unusual exchange. Usually we accept or take good things from others and in return we share our problems or worries. We tend to be selfish and defensive with a 'me first' attitude. With this practice we are putting the other first, yet strangely it is not at a cost to ourselves. It is not about being a martyr or about self-sacrifice. Rather, we recognise that our ordinary self is an illusion, a construct without essence, and so we can let it dissolve into the ocean of awareness without loss, and in fact, with the true gain of seeing how everything actually is. The wisdom of seeing this, of being this, is inseparable from compassion.

DIVERSE

As a small child I was anxious around people. I used to hate parties because at that time in Scotland children had to learn and perform 'a party piece', usually a song or a joke or a poem. Having to perform made me very self-conscious. I did not like to be visible as I felt it placed me apart in an unpleasant isolation. I remember going to a party in a classmate's flat when I was about seven. It must have been around Christmas time since they had a Christmas tree and after each child did their little song or whatever, they would get a present from the tree. But I felt too shy to do anything. At the end my mother came and collected me and as we walked off down the road I started crying because I didn't get my little present. So my mother said, *"Oh, we can go back and get your present."* So we went back to the boy's house and, although I did not have the qualities required to win my present, due to the blessing power of my mother I got my present and I was very happy. The mother of the boy whose party it was said, *"Yes, of course you can have this, James."* So it's the same now. From the very beginning our buddha potential is our present. We can have it anytime. But if we feel shy and lack the qualities to awaken by ourselves, then Padmasambhava will take our hand and make sure that we get our present. It's not all up to us.

The start of the meditation, our sense of the clear blue sky, offers a new beginning for everything. The middle part offers a further dispersal of the old, the solid, the seemingly enduring. The end of the meditation is rebirth in the unborn flow of becoming. This practice never ends.

We do not need to radically change our external behaviour, because as Patrul Rinpoche points out, what needs to shift is not the manner in which phenomena arise, but the manner in which they dissolve. That is to say, with our practice, life continues as usual, getting up, washing, going to the shops, cooking food, yet the particular space from which we engage in these activities is different. Whatever is arising, including our sense of self and other, is arising as the manifestation of the openness of our mind itself. The practice is called *dzogpa chenpo*, 'great perfection': by seeing the intrinsic purity or perfection of all phenomena we are released from our habitual impulse to control and improve events.

Relax, we are here, simply in the moment of shared revelation or co-emergence with others. Within this infinite non-duality we are spontaneous responsiveness as part of the precise moment.

When relating to others, if we can use their confusion and their limitations as fuel for our wisdom, then we'll be able to recognise their contribution and feel gratitude. This then allows us to be more generous towards them. With this they might experience the space in which they can relax from their identification with limited forms of identity. That's the theory. In practice, of course, it's slightly more difficult.

The buddhist view describes how we lose the open spaciousness of being, our original presence, when we collapse into false identification with momentary arisings as if these appearances were truly ourselves.

O penness reveals the unfixed moment, the space just before we speak or move or think or act. Are we going to arise and fill that moment on the basis of what we want to be there so that we close over the openness by knowing what the next moment will be in advance? Or are we going to relax and open and be here with whatever occurs? When we open rather than control we see that the ground space and what arises from it are not two different 'things'. Their non-duality reveals the pervasive indestructibility of space. Space is filled but not displaced for it is filled with its own radiance. Space and its radiance are neither the same nor different—they are non-dual. Being surprised by the world and by ourselves keeps life fresh and connected.

T antric practice helps to soften our sense of the world. This little wooden table in front of me is made of solid wood and it appears to be a hard entity, separate and existing in and of itself. The table and myself clearly appear to be two separate entities. The reality of the table is given by itself and similarly it appears that the separate reality of myself is intrinsic to me, yet both the table and myself are known to me through and as my experience of them. They are experiences for and in my mind. Their status is not self-existing but depends on my interpretation of my experience, and both interpretation and interpreted experience are mere transient reflections in the mirror of awareness. The describer and the interpreter and the judge all are ego functions and feel like me – but they are not the experiencer itself, which is pure, open, naked awareness. Rather than focussing always on the description of 'things' and their 'qualities', meditation points us towards finding out who is the actual experiencer of the experience. This is the one enquiry that frees everything.

In the view of Buddhism the heart of wisdom is openness or emptiness. Through attending to our own mental processes while being with others, we come to recognise the ways in which we construct our sense of other people and of ourself out of our own past experience, our own knowledge and our own fantasy projections. All of this illusory magical construction, which seems so real, occurs in fact within the space of the open empty mind.

In meditation we can start to be present at the moment when a thought arises. We see how we are instantly caught up in the thought as it arises, generating a feeling or a knowledge that 'I am angry' or 'I am tired' or 'I need to phone my mother.' I am sitting in the meditation and the thought arises, *"Blast! I haven't phoned my mother."* Now if my meditation is not very powerful, and since my mother *is* very powerful, I jump up for the telephone. If my meditation were a bit stronger I could put that thought on hold and just have a trace attention to the content of it but let the form of the thought pass through, knowing that, of course, I will think of my mother soon after. So what is the relationship between me, the thought and my mother? The thought is the vehicle for attachment, it is the glue that seems to bind these two seemingly separate entities, me and my mother together. Yet the thought vanishes. It vanishes without a trace, and the sense of my mother and of me in this moment also vanishes. This vanishing is effortless. When the impermanence and emptiness of the 'subject' is clear then our sky-like mind reveals itself.

In meditation we develop an attitude of openness and tenderness to our thoughts, and a similar capacity to receive the tenderness of the world. It is the tenderness of the world that supports us. If we have to do it all by ourselves, as if we were acting against the world, we will get exhausted. But our true strength arises from being able to work with the world as it moves around us and in us. We are enworlded, we are part of the world and that is our strength. Our thoughts come, not as our privately produced thoughts, but as the thoughts of the world passing through us. Being present in non-duality, all the strength and all the richness that we need is freely available for us.

When an existential fear arises, rather than turning away we should turn towards it, open to it and let it reveal what it actually is. When fear and anxiety arise they are so quickly wrapped in ideas, interpretations and assumptions that it is difficult to see the naked simplicity of what is occurring. If we encounter the wrapped up experience it can seem daunting and if we are to face it we often slip into hero mode. Then we face our foe and engage with it as our ego-self. Through this we can painfully gain qualities like patience and courage. This is useful. Yet from a dzogchen perspective our aim is not to be heroic but to be open like the sky. The sky lets everything pass through it – planes, storms, rainbows – they are there and then they are gone and the sky itself is untouched. The indestructible vajra mind is like the empty spacious sky – it accepts all without struggle, reservation or bias.

When we practise basic shine or shamatha, we focus exclusively on our breath. We yoke the horse of our intention to the plough of our attention and align it with the little double furrow at our nostrils. Then we just keep the plough steady and unwavering. So how many people here were able to plough in a straight line for fifteen minutes?

With our usual ordinary sense of duality, everything that we do in the world and everything that happens to us is an affirmation of the substantial reality of phenomena. This, fortunately or unfortunately, is a fantasy arising from ignorance. When we are successful, when we are unsuccessful, when we are happy, when we are sad, every experience, every action that we do, is taken as proof that subject and object are real and separate. This is why the texts say that samsara is endless. We ourselves are maintaining the flow of misinformation, misinterpretation and confusion. If we do not see what we are up to this non-sense will go on and on. But if we look carefully and see how we take our assumptions to be facts we can start to question the seeming truth of our beliefs. Seeing that they are constructs, we can see that all that appears for us is essenceless illusion. This is most helpful.

However, deep and vast awakening occurs when we see that we ourselves, the subject, the thinker, the knower, the doer, are in fact also just patterns of experience in our own mind. My 'self', my 'identity' is a sequence of patterning of evanescent energy which is the play of my mind. So what is my mind? Where is it? How is it? This is the big door, the ever-open door, the door to freedom that has always been with us. Finding it directly and going through it with no hesitancy or caveat and not turning back or looking for something else—this is the origin of dzogchen in our world. This is the gift of Garab Dorje's three statements: be open, don't doubt, stay open.

Prayer is a method which uses the structure of dualistic separation to intensify the energy of longing so that our ordinary self and the divine form can start to vibrate and come together revealing our own emptiness. After praying with great faith and receiving the light of the four initiations, Padmasambhava comes to the top of your head evoking warm feelings in your heart. Then he folds into a ball of light and descends into your heart. You are aware of this radiant presence coming into you, very deep inside you. All that you have ever wanted, all that you have ever longed for in another person, in another object, is now present as this radiant presence inside your heart. You open fully to it and dissolve in it. Then the non-dual single ball of light shrinks to a point and dissolves. There is only openness, emptiness. Resting in this spaciousness, appearances gradually manifest. Appearance manifests from space, as the display of space, and is not essentially different from space. In this way all that occurs is Padmasambhava.

True healing is to wake up to the integrated three aspects of the mind, openness, clarity and responsivity. This heals by cutting through basic ignorance which is the root of the five poisons, of attachment, and of all the sufferings that arise.

If we have sufficient factors around us which prop us up we seem to be okay. Yet it's like a magician's sleight of hand. We easily and effortlessly delude ourselves into thinking that we're grounded when actually we're impulsive and reactive and truly unstable. We are not unstable because we are bad or lazy but because all phenomena are impermanent.

Our sense of self often carries the sense that we are a fixed 'thing', a substantial essence. However, if we look at how we actually are, we see that we are not fixed or definable. Our 'self' is an ongoing 'selfing', a dynamic interactive disclosure of the potential of our being which is open, empty, and always available. Self-referential selfing is like editing a narrative, a way of organising the moments of experience into a seemingly coherent story which confirms the continuity and integrity of our 'self'. However, our 'self' is not self-existing but is formed moment by moment with the thoughts we have which self-reflexively confirm our 'self' as something already existing. We are all caught up in this activity of self-construction and its allied practice of ignoring the fact of construction and pretending that we have a continuous existence as a real entity. The huge amount of editing involved in this keeps our attention well away from the open ground of being. Social politeness means that we tolerate slippages in other peoples' narratives — *"I won't tell you you're incoherent if you don't tell me I'm incoherent!"* This keeps the drama of the individual centre-stage in a non-stop production.

By looking carefully we can see how, when we identify with and merge into the thoughts and feelings which then feel like 'me', we engage in a process of constituting or creating our sense of self. These thoughts are not mirrors or x-rays that show me who I actually am. They are the building blocks of who I actually am, as I take myself to be. It is through merging with the thoughts of 'I' and 'me' that I, my open potential, become 'me'. With this clarity we can turn towards seeing who is this 'I' when I don't think about it.

Buddhism indicates something very disturbing and very radical. The texts point out that we are asleep within a dream within which we take a part of our potential to be the whole. This dream is constructed out of a particular set of causes and events. Due to having created causes in the past, we have come to be born in this human dimension, sharing a particular kind of karma with other humans. This seemingly shared vision supports our belief that the delusion is real and so distracts us from enquiry. After a while, the causal forces which generate our access to this domain will be exhausted and then we will find ourselves in another domain, another hologram, another arena of experience – and it probably won't be as nice. So we need awaken from the dream world of samsara.

There is no one true rulebook that can tell you how to live. We are all flying by the seat of our pants. In this situation it's best to keep your eyes open, your ears open, your heart open and stay in the dance. Of course there are many rulebooks that can tell us what to do in general but our lives are not lived 'in general'. We are exquisitely located in time and space with the unique specificity of each moment of our lives. Only we see through our eyes – to accept this reveals the ego's world to be a lonely one. We can try to avoid this fact by utilising shared generalities yet our specificity is unique. Maps and rulebooks can give us the sense of knowing about something prior to experiencing it. Yet our lived experience is of being here in this fresh situation and having to respond within the dynamic unfolding. So, will we trust the maps we have been given or shall we attend to the fresh actuality and participate as embodied non-duality? If we choose the latter way we come to trust that we find our way by walking in the world as it shows itself.

In order to develop we need to find a way to inhabit the tension which always exists between our desire for excitement, creativity, expansion and new possibilities on the one hand, and our need for comfort, reassurance, and security on the other. The key is not to invest any situation or possibility with a sense of ultimate value. Everything matters and does not matter simultaneously.

The flow of my experience ceaselessly occurs. I can be open to the flow as something apart from awareness or as the participative field of awareness. Thoughts, feelings and sensations arise from emptiness, in emptiness, as emptiness. Tasting without grasping reveals that every moment is rich and fresh. When there is nothing to be done we rest in awareness, unruffled by any of the forms which occur. This is the primordial purity of the mind, kadag. When there is a need, in the manner of a dream we emerge as energy patterns in the field of clarity. This is non-dual co-emergence, compassion free of reification, the instant presence of the potential of awareness, lhundrup. Unchanging purity and instant presence are inseparable.

The dzogchen view points out that attachment arises from a dualistic orientation, from setting up oppositional categories, the poles of which appear to be both truly existing and fundamentally different. The most basic of these polarities is that of self and other, belief in which generates the sense that I exist apart from others and apart from the environment around me. Once this is established hope for gain and fear of loss become the organising principles for engagement with all that is deemed other.

Rather than the mind being a possession of the self, the self is a construct of the mind. When we don't realise this, the openness or potentiality of the mind is ignored through a decontextualising reification of appearance and our grasping at the manifestations of the creativity of the mind including our 'self'.

The heart of the meditation practice is the subtle work of re-balancing our habitual bias towards our ego sense of self. This bias gives our feelings of individuality a sense of importance and centrality which it does not actually have. Paradoxically our true centre cannot be found for it is our unborn spacious awareness, present everywhere yet forever eluding capture.

When we meditate by opening to whatever occurs, it is at first a bit like speed dating. In speed dating, many strangers come together in their search for love. They have five minutes sitting in pairs to meet and introduce themselves. Then they move on to the next person. Will I find my one true love? In meditation we want to find who we truly are. So we interview all the candidates who present themselves. Thought after thought comes in front of us, intriguing, enticing, fascinating and beguiling. 'Love me!' they say, 'Merge with me! I am all you have been looking for.' And then they are gone and the next one appears and says the same old line. All talk and no trousers. Sweet words and then goodbye. Well, if we want enduring love we need to settle for the mind itself and not go chasing after these charming but oh so deceitful temptations.

Clothes show themselves when you put them on. If a dress is hanging in a wardrobe, you don't truly know what it's like. You have to take it out and hold it up, and even then you don't know if it is right for you at this moment. To find that out you have to put it on. It is only when you wear it that the garment can reveal itself along with your current mood in relation to it. In the same way the nature and status of subject and object are not revealed by abstract thought. When we open to our experience in the here and now, moment by moment, then we find that 'self' and 'other' are being draped over what is occurring. Now you can see if they fit and if they are needed. We tend to wear too many clothes, we are all covered up in habits, memories, old stuff that has been in the wardrobe of our mind for too long. Being present in the freshness of our mind as it shows itself, we gain the confidence to be naked and unadorned. This is Kuntuzangpo, our naked being, the bodying forth of the dharmadhatu. This dharmakaya only wears clothes for the benefit of others – new outfits arise without effort as required. Self and other, good and bad – these styles are way out of fashion in Buddhaland.

The tumbling experience of being ourselves arises in relation to the environment. The more we open in a fresh way with the environment as it shows itself the less stable we will become. This is the heart of the dzogchen teaching: we cannot control our self-identity. Our self is part of the world and it will change as the world changes. So let it change, and instead find stillness where stillness always already is.

Rather than changing the object which arises, whether it seems good or bad, we are simply loosening the bond of identification and attachment. This bond is made by us, not by the qualities of the object. The sweet taste of freedom is already ours, if we wish it.

On this essential point of recognising our true presence, there is nothing to recognise. It is not an object and it is not a cognition. We don't get anything, we don't find anything and neither do we recognise anything. Our presence is not something which we can lose or get. It is not an object to be found nor is it a quality of the subject to be developed. Relaxing the anxious fixation driving dualistic perception, we find ourselves in unborn awareness. We don't dissolve into nothing at all, we don't vanish completely. Rather we, the reflection, in giving up the delusion that we are a substance, find ourselves in and as the mirror. The falsity of self-construction fades like morning mist and the clarity of non-duality allows us to see ourselves when there is nothing to see and no one to see it.

The problem of the subject cannot be solved by the object. Our confusion, the difficulties we feel, our uncertainties about who we are, and about the meaning of our life, will not be resolved by finding the perfect object and falling in love. The lovely other may enable you to have a holiday from the difficulty of being yourself but after a while you will find that the difficulty is still here. That's why we have to learn to be with ourselves, with our thoughts and feelings and find the way to let them lead us to our own true being.

We exist in the world, as part of the world, and the world reveals itself to us through our participation. We are revealed to ourselves and to others, through our participation. There are two paths open to us, participation as a separate individual or participation as a non-dual part of the unfolding field.

Meditation practice can gradually change the content of our mind but, much more importantly, it will change the relationship we have with the content of our mind. Meditation can be very boring and this can assist us to be less and less fascinated by and dependent upon the content of experience. As our thoughts and feelings are seen for what they are, our lessening interest lets us start to taste awareness free of content. This does not mean that there is no content. The content is still there, just as before, but our simple awareness is untouched by it.

The clarity which is produced by thoughts is developed by linking one thought to another thought. But the clarity which arises from relaxation, openness and emptiness, is present prior to thought. Thoughts arise as the shiny edge of this awareness, as if you are looking at the sea in the moonlight and the edges of the breaking waves shimmer with a silvery sheen. Our thoughts are like little drops of spray, of beautiful energy arising from the open dharmakaya ocean. They are the ceaseless display of our mind's own luminous potential.

Our buddha potential is something that we can trust. The problem is that we are out of touch with it. Something has to shift so that we can connect with our true being. To change gear from samsara to nirvana we need to use the clutch of emptiness. At the moment we are locked in the gear of our karmic identity, driving along at this particular speed, perceiving what we perceive at this speed. However, making use of emptiness, we can change gear, and now we are travelling in mandala mode and everything that appears is Padmasambhava.

The essential point is very simple. Don't take life too seriously. If you look back, you will see that you have already had many troubles in the past, and now they have gone. Now you are struggling with the problems of this moment, and if you are lucky enough to stay alive, they will be replaced by new problems in the future. So don't take your current problems too seriously – they are not the end of the line.

The mind of the deity is emptiness, the open, unlimited, pure awareness which is the ground of everything. Everything arises within this mind. This mind is not something moving towards objects as if they were external to it, but is the very cornucopia, the very womb of existence, within which subject and object carry on their eternal play.

Learn to relax the body, releasing muscular tension and the formality of self-presentation. Learn to allow speech to flow freely, releasing editing and blocking, staying present in interpersonal responsiveness. Learn to trust the unborn openness of your mind, releasing identification with thoughts, feelings, memory and all that may arise.

Practise letting go of your attachments, opening to your connection with others and settling into the intrinsic spaciousness of your being.

When we relate directly to our own experience we start to see the infinity of the revelation of the integrated movement of subject and object. That is to say, the root quality of our alive intelligence, our awareness, is something ungraspable. It has no personal or private content of its own which is always there, but is rather a potential within which infinite forms can be revealed.

Is nothing better than something? That is the key question. We have to be clear for ourselves. Is the yogi who spends her life in a cave wasting her life? In the midst of 'nothing' is everything; in the midst of 'something' is disappointment.

Rather than seeing our ordinary lives as something stable, secure and reliable, through the practice of meditation we come to experience our mind as the flow of ungraspable experience within open, empty, mirror-like spaciousness. This shift may well feel alarming. What about the reassurance we derive from object constancy and repetition compulsion? If I give up the seeming reliability of the forms and patterns I cling to, my assumptions will fade, my automatic responses will slow down and I will not know how to act or be myself. How can this be an improvement? Well, the complacency we have been operating with is only effective when the environment supports it. All patterns are vulnerable to change. Our ego, our personality, our sense of self – these are all essenceless patterns vulnerable to shifts in circumstances. Seeing that this is the case we might seek for what is truly reliable. The surprising and strange fact is that the most reliable aspect of existence is its emptiness. The absence of self-substance in appearances is the basis for liberation from the deluding fantasy of stable reliable entities.

Within and through our own basic openness free of inherent content, all movement, all gesture, all experience reveals itself, moment by moment, as the specificity of transient this or transient that. In this way our participation in the world is part of the flow of emergent energy. This is our aliveness for we are no longer operating on automatic pilot. We are not taking things for granted. We are touched and moved by the freshness of our contact with the living world. Subject and object ceaselessly dance, creating infinite patterns while our mind itself, our true awareness is calm, clear and unruffled.

Having no fixed shape itself, when our awareness reveals particular patterned moments, it is as if our awareness (mistaken as an enduring personal identity) is in fact the current content of our mind. In that moment it is as if we, our unborn awareness, are our jealousy, our pride, our laziness, our diligence. There is no substantial basis for this seeming merging, identification and attachment. A reflection appears to be in the mirror, and in a way it is, although it was not put into the mirror nor can it be taken out of the mirror. Similarly, thoughts are in our mind and can appear to be our mind, yet they are neither the same as the mind nor different. Therefore it is vital not to react to a transient content of the mind as if it were self or not-self. Involvement is the work of dualistic consciousness. It brings no true benefit and confuses us as to how our mind truly is. So, rest in the intrinsic integration of awareness and its self-display since forgetfulness of the open ground allows mind's energy to appear substantial, and this creates all aspects of samsara.

It is the quality of awareness to reveal what is here, and what is here is the energy of awareness. If we are not present as awareness itself our awareness will simply reveal the manifesting qualities of the transient formations of dualised subject (which we identify with) and object (which we like or don't like). The aspect of energy which is our involving ego consciousness will grasp onto whatever it is in contact with without seeing that these 'objects' are also aspects of our mind's energy. For example, if in meditation we think, *"Oh no, I am too tired, I can't do this!"* this is because tiredness seems to be all that is present. Illuminating awareness, the source, is not attended to and so clarity displays itself as us being lost in fusion with whatever is arising.

When we feel overwhelmed the object or situation feels big, and we, the subject, feel small. We, the subject, feel vulnerable and unstable and the object-situation we encounter seems to be powerful and inevitable. We are sure that we are going to be crushed, we are sure that we can't survive. The only true exit from this delusion lies in meditation. We need to trust the truth of emptiness and release our reification and our fear. Keep relaxing in the face of whatever arises and it will dissolve in front of us. The power of the object is the power of our mind – so why are we giving it to the object?

When you listen to the dharma try to experience the words as droplets of rain gently falling on you and washing away all your doubts and confusions. In particular, as you listen to sentences being formed, you can see the various grammatical particles in operation together. This co-dependency, interdependency or dependent co-origination is very obvious in language, as each part of the sentence plays its role in bringing something into being. Attending to this we can start to feel directly the energetic quality of words as they impact the various centres in our body. The fact that language itself—something so fleeting and so inter-dependent—seems to support the notion of real entities is really quite amazing.

If dzogchen is saying *"All things from the very beginning are pure,"* and we are saying, *"No, I have some really bad thoughts, I'm really horrible. I don't want anybody to know this about me."* This would indicate that we are excluding ourselves from our own intrinsic purity. The fact that other people might agree with us that indeed our qualities are terrible would then offer us a chance to make use of their limits to reaffirm our limits. Worldly opinion confirms limits as real while meditation reveals the illusory quality of limits.

In our practice we are open to the fact that everything is pure yet when we are in the world with others we also need to be careful. Dzogchen doesn't mean that you should be naive. Although all the patterns of experience are truly empty illusions, patterns can and do bump into each other with painful results. So until you can see that pain is also an illusion it is best to take care.

At Halloween children dress up as ghosts and demons and go out knocking on people's doors. They put on masks or paint their faces and go 'Wooh!' They want to be very terrifying but really they are just sweet little children. It is the same with these thoughts which look so terrible and seem so unbearable. Actually, they are just the sweet children of emptiness; they are the children of the dharmakaya. When you observe thoughts from this point of view, they are a shining radiance even though they may appear to be dull or disturbing. The 'shining radiance' quality is not the semantic or overt content, it is the clarity intrinsic to the energy of display as it moves within the field of awareness. Clarity is the relationship of manifestation with its own ground of emptiness. So however experience is, whatever is occurring, remain relaxed, open and uninvolved.

Don't despair if your mind seems very dull. This dullness doesn't mean that you are far away from your unborn awareness. The fact that you experience being alive and are cognisant of this dullness is itself the intrinsic radiance of the unborn mind.

One day when I was doing chod practice in Ladakh, I was sitting outside my little tent writing something down on the wrapping paper of a packet of incense sticks. I always write a lot and I had run out of paper. My tent was pitched in a little cremation ground quite far from the nearest village but a lama came striding across the stones and looked at me sitting there writing. He picked up two stones and banged them together saying strongly, "*Stones are better than words, they won't cause you so much trouble.*" Then he shot off again. He was a very helpful lama. Our habitual fascination with particular ideas, our efforts to freeze the moment or capture our own thoughts which seem to be so very important—these are dangerous blind-spots for meditators.

The Buddha said that suffering arises from attachment. Attachment is our effort to hang on to our idea of something so that we believe we can move it from the past into the present and on into the future. Of course it is not the object itself we are moving, only our ideas about it. Yet due to our attachment to duality, the object as it is and our idea about it have been conflated. In the moment of our attachment we forget that there is no truth to any object, no inherent reality to any object. The seasons change, languages change, national boundaries change, the body changes, thoughts and feelings change. Suffering arises because we resist being with how things actually are.

The function of meditation is to enter into the ceaseless flow of live experience. It is not about controlling or improving or getting rid of things but of finding one's balance like a surfer, staying with the waves of experience as they roll on and on.

The energy of the mind is ceaseless and we can't grasp even one moment of our experience. What we get when we grasp is an idea or a concept which seems to stand for the experience itself. Confusing these aspects is delusion. We are like a little mouse in a cage, on one of those wheels going round and round and round. The more the mouse tries to get somewhere, the more it stays in the same place. There is nowhere to get to. *"But if I am not making something of my life what will happen to me? It will all fall apart and then where will I be? It is all up to me. If I don't take care of me who is going to do it?"* These anxious thoughts keep us running on the wheel.

In all situations just stay present in the centre of what is occurring without losing your balance. Allow whatever arises to arise, confident that it will pass. In this way, one is working with the teachings of the Buddha.

What is asleep is not the presence of the mind but the content of the mind. When a thought arises in the mind and we believe the thought, who is the one who believes the thought? If you observe yourself, you start to see how a thought believes a thought – a thought follows a thought, followed by another thought. That is what samsara is. You are caught up in thoughts and thoughts catch you—on and on and on.

The whole art of life is to release and relax, letting go into the timeless present.

Compassion is awakening to the actuality of our connection with others. This is always already here, present even before we're aware of it. Compassion's quality is connectivity.

We stand at the crossroads directing good things towards us and bad things away from us. There is a lot of traffic, a lot of fumes and the pay of a traffic policeman is not so good.

The only place you can get lost is in your own energy. What hides us from ourselves is ourselves. The energy of the mind in the richness of its display is so dazzling that we forget that we are also the ground of that display.

There is continuity in our lives, but it is a continuity of change. Since we were children everything has changed in our lives. Our thoughts and feelings have changed so often, the shapes of our bodies have changed, the kinds of activities we do have changed. So what is the continuity of our identity? It is some sort of felt sense of 'here-I-am', but here I am as what? As 'this' in the morning, and as 'that' in the afternoon. The content of 'what I am' and 'how I am' is changing, changing, and changing. Recognising the empty quality of everything including ourselves is wisdom, for it frees us from false attribution and allows us to experience what is occurring without avoidance, merging, attachment or bias. Experiencing form as inseparable from emptiness is compassion since we see how sentient beings wrongly take illusory forms to be substantial entities and in doing so generate great suffering for themselves and others.

We don't look at the world the way a camera takes an impression. We look at the world through our values, our beliefs and assumptions, our likes and dislikes. Something may be very attractive to some people and not very attractive to others. We don't simply say, "I like this cheese" which would indicate our relationship to it, but we say, "This is a really good cheese." In this way the 'goodness' seems to be inherent in the object. However for someone else it might be a very 'bad' cheese. Our 'truth' is only an opinion, only the view from here.

The root of who we are is awareness inseparable from emptiness, and this emptiness is the basis of the ceaseless flow of our experience. If we settle into this awareness, we will find that it is more reliable than any friend. Whenever we look for our mind it will be there, yet we will never find it as a substantial entity. Friendships form and change. If your friends didn't change, their lives would be very limited – but these very changes alter their availability. As the Buddha said, *"Friends become enemies, and enemies become friends."* We can go through life telling ourselves stories about how the world is in order to make our world feel safe, but this is merely to fall asleep in illusion. The only unchanging refuge is our own true buddha potential.

Relax into your own ground, the intrinsic perfection of your own presence. Experience its limitless infinity and see directly that it is the ground, source and field of all experience. This is your home territory. This is where you belong. So why not relax and enjoy it?

One of the functions of buddhist understanding and practice is to start to see the cocoon of assumptions within which we live. The more we understand the nature of the cocoon, and that we ourselves have spun it, the more we free ourselves from it. In that way we go from being a little grub to being a lovely butterfly. Beautiful!

Looking in front of me I can see another person yet I can't see my own shape very clearly. I can bend and see under the other person's chin, but even if I did yoga for fifty years I would never be able to see under my own chin. This indicates that other people are more visible to us than we are to ourselves. Similarly they see us more clearly than we do. In fact we need other people to see ourselves, to see how we are and what we are up to. The sangha is the field of collaboration in which we all engage in learning.

We are not a fixed thing. We are not a coherent self. What we take to be ourself is an aspect of the flow of experience we encounter. Tendencies, traits, and memories move together creating different patterns, like dancers on a stage. The various aspects of ourselves are energies moving in the background like a corps de ballet, and then suddenly one of these aspects decides to be the prima ballerina and goes out to take centre stage. This is great when the moment is ripe but the 'star' needs to be able to rejoin the corps de ballet. When an aspect of our potential becomes a permanent star we will be off balance.

If we use the simile that our world is like a piece of sculpture, then each of the nine yanas or vehicles functions as a different angle of illumination of the sculpture. When you look from each viewpoint the sculpture shows a particular aspect which, in this moment of looking, appears to be the truth of the sculpture. You can walk around the sculpture looking from each of these nine different viewpoints, and each view is just what you get from that specific position. One view is not better or worse than any other view. In meditation practice we are the sculpture, simultaneously simple and complex. It helps not to get stuck in just one way of viewing. Yet we should avoid comparing and contrasting and be fully committed to whatever view we are currently entertaining.

Thoughts are like politicians. Politicians always say, *"Trust me. I speak the truth. I will work for your benefit."* Watch out for these inner politicians. Simply observe how thoughts arise and pass. Just as politicians say so many sweet things before an election and then afterwards don't do very much, these thoughts seem very attractive when they are arising, but then they are gone.

Buddhism offers ways of awakening from our dream of solidity. This doesn't mean that we leave the sense of things being strongly real and enter a mere nothingness. Rather we stop over-investing the fleeting moment and remain open and present. Then moment-by-moment we can experience the world directly as the play of our mind.

If you think *"I have understood"* you put the Buddha in your pocket to keep him safe, but later when you look in your pocket you only find a rotting apple. Whatever is turned into a 'thing' will change and rot. The way to use dharma is not to take it so seriously but to actively use it to soften your rigid beliefs.

Each of us has to decide whether to continue to build our identity from limited concepts, or to open to the teachings and explore directly who we are. Limiting concepts can be comforting in their familiarity yet they diminish our availability to the ceaseless hospitality of our own unborn nature. Observe how many small worlds you have already invested your time and energy in. Recollect how they have all vanished. Your true friend and ally is not far away. In fact, if you stop being so busy and stop looking so hard you will find that what you need is already here.

Not tilting away from occurrences, not tilting towards them, simply staying present with everything as it occurs – this is the heart of meditation.

In meditation, the more we can let go the better it is, whereas in the world the more we can accumulate the better it is. This does not mean that you have to practise renunciation of external phenomena. Rather, by relaxing into openness again and again, you come to see the dynamic, impermanent nature of illusory forms, both subject and object. With this we can freely participate in the unfolding matrix of the world without too many hopes and fears.

On an ordinary level our lives are constructed on the arrow of time and on the basis of cause and effect. Whereas the paths of direct experience take us into the heart of time, an infinite moment that has no beginning and no end.

We are asleep in the dream of duality. The actuality of non-duality continues to be the case even while we are asleep and dreaming of many different things. The sense of being a separate self is a dream formation that vanishes upon awakening. Our buddha potential is outside of time. It is not conditioned by any of the events that occur in time, for linear time is always dream time.

Space is open and unmoving even while winds move through space. In the same way in the open mirror, reflections come and go, yet the mirror itself doesn't move. Our buddha potential is like space. It is not something hidden inside us. It is not something to discover in the future when we are ready. It is not something we had in the past and then lost. It is simply the basis of experience moment by moment, experience as the non-dual arising of self and field.

In dzogchen, nothing can spoil meditation other than being somewhere else.

This is the work: to allow whatever arises to come and go, and, simultaneously, to stay relaxed and open as spacious awareness free of reified essence and definition.

The deeper the meditation goes, the more unformed and infinite we experience ourselves to be. This liberates our playful energy. With increased clarity, we see situations more easily. It then is important to be precise and careful in everything we do, harmonious, attuned, soft and with a lightness of touch.

Recognise that from the very beginning our being is pure. I am not a thing. I am not an entity. How I am is ungraspable, like the sky. This infinite openness gives rise to all phenomena. Resting in openess that allows phenomena to come and go, the distorted ego-winds gradually dissolve and there is clarity and spaciousness. From clarity and spacious-ness a deep satisfaction arises, a contentment which means you have no need to go and do things. You can just sit quietly and not be so hungry for experience.

To be alive is a very individual thing. We're not homogenised, we're not clones of each other. Respecting the unique specificity of others is very important in dzogchen. We're not trying to control other people and make them the way we want them to be. Rather, we experience their vibrant ever-changing patterning as an encouragement to relax into the flow as part of the flow.

Dzogchen is not much concerned with getting your life sorted. Whether you're serious or you're foolish, whether you have a settled life or a crazy life, whether you are rich or poor—none of these things impact the rela-tionship with the ground. Everything arises from the ground. Everything has the same quality or, in the language of mahamudra, everything has one taste. This is the taste of emptiness. When you taste that one taste, the forms of life do not matter so much. You can relax and let your life arise according to circumstances.

In buddhism, as in all religions, dreams of power have led many people astray. Power can be dangerous. Since the ground of power is emptiness, if we have an authentic compassionate intention, power may be useful. But it's very easy to fall in love with power and to let its impetus carry us along. So, again and again, we should question: 'What is our motivation in doing practice?' 'What is our motivation when we interact with other people?'

Our existence is structured in two modes: the host and the guest. The guests come and go; the host is always there. The host can neither be grasped nor defined. The guests can be briefly encountered yet not grasped. We all know what's it's like to feel sad or lonely, we know what it's like to feel happy, we know what it's like to feel full of energy and eager to work. Each of these fleeting mental states can be known—they have a particular shape—but the one who receives and illuminates these passing guests has no form or shape that can be grasped. The indefinable unlimited host has nothing to gain or lose from any guest and so is even and hospitable to all.

M ovement is the energy of stillness. Stillness and movement are non-dual. They are not oppositional, and they are not enemies. Neither is trying to block or inhibit or destroy the other. That which is still, spacious and open, is in fact inseparable from all the movement that arises from it and in it.

W e are not the owners of our open being, but rather we are the children of our open being. The domain of I, me, myself is an energetic arising. It's not a problem to be solved nor is it something to be removed. However, the energy patterns of myself need to settle back and be held safely in the arms of their mother. The mother is space. The truth of our awareness, the ground of our existence, is open spaciousness without corners or edges. Without beginning or end our mother is always here, open and available. Lost and lonely as we can often feel, we have actually never left her hospitable womb.

Y ou can renounce external phenomena. You can give up your house, you can give up your money. You can become a monk or a nun. However, for meditators the central point of renunciation is to renounce the belief that the meaning of existence is to be found in concepts.

W hat we have is a path of open availability, which means being willing to not know in advance of emergent events. It's not about changing one belief system for another. It's not about becoming a buddhist. But it is about learning how to look clearly and simply at what is actually happening here and now.

Many of the difficulties that come in dharma practice arise because we ask the ego to do things it cannot do. The mind and the content of the mind are not the same. The ego is a content of the mind. The content can't do what the mind can do. The content of the mind is always smaller than the mind itself. To ask twenty people to sit on one chair would be silly. To ask the ego to be free of grasping is silly. Rather than spending time trying to transcend your ego-limits, enter into the openness free of limits.

The basis of dzogchen practice is to find oneself in the relaxed, intrinsic openness of awareness. This openness is not something far away. It is not a state dependent on causes and conditions, the way water can be in a hot state or a cold state. It is vital that we remember that the non-dual actuality is beyond language. Linguistics signs are at best evocative – they cannot truly indicate how it is. Awareness is not something mystical or esoteric. It is always here but it is hidden by its own brilliance. The radiance of your own mind—which arises as the continuous stream of thoughts, feelings and expressions—is such a dazzling display that you are blinded to your own invisible being.

Thoughts come and go in the spaciousness of the mind. Speech arises and passes in the spaciousness of silence. Movement occurs and vanishes in the spaciousness of stillness. In this way, whatever we are doing or experiencing is precisely as it is, never cut off from the field of arising inseparable from the all-integrating source.

It is very important to precisely understand what is meant in buddhism by the term 'illusion'. Perhaps a better way of translating it would be 'ungraspability'. The seeming solidity and reliability of phenomena is an illusion since they have no enduring self-substance. Both the grasper and the grasped are illusion. To see the emptiness of the object but still to hold on to the seeming substantial reality of the subject merely takes us further from liberation.

Problems exist in two domains, as event and as narrative. As an event problems have a beginning, a middle, and an end. As part of a narrative they can appear to be endless. The less we enter into absorption in the ego's narratives the more we are fresh with phenomena as they manifest momentarily. Clarity free of reification illuminates our activity and all phenomena are self-liberating effulgence.

The function of the practice has nothing to do with becoming a buddhist. It doesn't matter if you call yourself a buddhist or not. 'Buddhist' is a name and we already have a lot of names. The main point is to enquire, 'Who is the one who is here? What is this arising?' This is the path to enduring value.

Prince Siddhartha was shocked by encountering the sick, the old, the dead and the holy. Subsequently observing life in the palace where he lived, he started to see that things were not quite what they appeared to be. He was looking with fresh eyes and was troubled by what he saw.

So he left the palace and spent many years practising different kinds of meditation, many kinds of self-restraint, diminishing the amount of food he ate, holding postures for a very long time and so on. But after six years he found that these practices were not bringing fundamental change. He decided that he needed just to sit and be with himself. He wouldn't move until he had awakened to the truth of existence.

Paradoxically, by doing nothing, everything was achieved. Up until that point he had been pushing himself. But now he was just sitting still and breathing in and out. Thoughts and feelings were arising and passing, yet he was not involved in them. With equanimity to whatever occurred he was able to see that both subject and object were without inherent self-essence. With this clarity he was invulnerable to desire and aversion and all the other distracting forces which had previously blocked his path. Being with what is, rather than fusing with arisings or striving for something else is the middle way that he found and taught.

Nowadays many people seem to have an inner desolation and lack a sense of meaning. That is clearly not a healthy place to be. Now, because we tend to believe that the best places are far away and that deep down we are unworthy, it may make sense to engage in a practice that will prepare us to be able to go somewhere better. This will give us a sense of purpose. Yet by acting in that way we can avoid attending to our actual situation. Attention to what is brings calm clarity while judgement about what is here will mobilise us to restlessly seek a transient something better elsewhere.

The ego-self is very fragile. Happiness is easily lost. We built our house on sand. The various factors which continue to give us the sense of who we are don't fit together all that easily. Just saying, 'I exist, I exist' doesn't really give us a certainty. Chasing experience will lead us astray. Who is the one who is aware of the thought, the feeling, the sensation? This enquiry reveals the intrinsic purity and clarity of the mind itself.

This world is meaningless. We give meaning to the world. The meanings which seem to exist out there are all projected. Rather than exploring the meanings we take to be embedded in the world we would be better off exploring the true source of these meanings.

Don't ask thoughts to do what they can't do. Thoughts are fragile; they don't live very long and they can't do very much. Although there is no end to thinking, thoughts never establish anything reliable. We, however, use these thoughts to create the whole world. Every day we are busy constructing this great edifice of samsara with our thoughts. Thoughts are very young, they like to play, so let them play. The point is, don't ask your thoughts to give you the meaning of existence. They cannot do that. Don't ask them to do what they can't do.

When life is hard it is difficult to trust that awakening is easy.

Tantra is a path of activity, and one of its strengths is that it gives us something to do. There are mudras to form with your hands, a dorje and bell to hold, instruments to play, texts to read, and many images to visualise. The beauty and skilful organisation of these patterns of movement allow such a focus of attention that no aspect of our mind is left free to be caught up in distraction. In tantra you are working with energy, with the transformation of your experience of what is occurring. However in dzogchen one is concerned simply to relax into the intrinsic purity of open presence and let energy come as it comes.

In the practice of tantra, the orientating view is that from the very beginning nothing has truly existed. Visualised images are arising moment by moment. These images are translucent, playful, and essentially delightful, but if you grasp them in the wrong way they turn into sharp, hot objects that will burn and cut you. It's about how you take the world. It's about having a lightness of touch.

The term 'dependent co-arising' points to the co-emergence of all the factors in the field. Every arising is linked to every other arising and they are mutually influencing. Thus 'how I am' is called forth by how you are. Who I am is not defined by something inside me, but is the shimmering surface, the interface between subject and object. We emerge in interaction, and the ground of both subject and object is ungraspable, beyond thought, word and expression. Our practice is to attend to the immediacy of how we and our world appear in this moment rather than going in search of an imagined essence.

WE CAN HAVE IT ALL

What we seek is happiness,
Contentment, relaxation.
Not finding this we seek
Stimulus, change, excitation.

Active engagement generates
Our sense of self
Self maintained by
Active engagement.

No need for more activity
No need to stop activity
Activity occurs, certainly, constantly –
So who is the doer?

Neither merging nor observing
Be present at the site of activity.
The action passes,
The actor dissolves.

Neither looking back nor forward
Be present here and now where life is happening.
Life flows, the moment goes,
Ungraspable presence is changeless.

Life goes on, round and round
Hopes and fears, up and down
Wave upon wave
Yet depth and space are unruffled.

Stillness and contentment
Movement and change
Non-dual, without contradiction
No loss, no gain; complete.

When we truly see that everything is passing, we awaken to the fact that the evanescent moment can only be enjoyed, it cannot be grasped. There is no doggy bag for experience, we don't take anything away. Our karma might go with us, being the patterning which constitutes us, yet if we release the site of identification and appropriation, everything goes free. The main function of meditation in dzogchen is simply to release, release, and release. The central point is relaxation, not striving.

Dzogchen is primordial. It has no history. Yet there are histories of how these teachings came into the world. Dzogchen is intrinsic to all beings – but transmission is required to awaken to it. It is not an invented system, but is the presence that was, and is, and always will be here. All beings, in all places, in all times, can have access to it since dzogchen is their own true presence.

Our body is not a thing, it's a great river of change. The same is true for sensations and feelings and thoughts. Once we start to experience the ceaseless movement of experience we realise that within this movement there is nothing to hold on to. Yet we don't get lost, for the ground of this movement is completely still and always precisely here and now.

Movement is never still. You cannot make it still. The only thing that is still is the presence of awareness, our unchanging true being.

W e can tell closed stories or open stories. We can have the story of the expert person or the story of the pathetic person. Best of all, however, is the story that we tell with other people, a story which is allowed to emerge as a conversation allowing us to find out that we are always fresh.

I find myself by being with you. I don't find myself inside myself but I am revealed through being with you. I am revealed now as this one who is being with you. I am not revealed as the real me because there is no 'real me'. The more aspects of you that you show me the more aspects of me will be shown to you and to me.

T he more relaxed and open I am the easier it is to have a sense of all of you who are here with me today. By having a sense of you all, I can speak with you. The ground of our coming into being with the other is not a fixed recipe from a book. It is not a thing inside us but is the relaxing of our defences and the lessening of the intensity of our self-definition. In this way we become at ease with the negative capability of not knowing. This profound not knowing is itself the door to 'wisdom'. Not knowing gives us access to the knowing which is present prior to thinking. It is not dependent on thinking nor is it based on expelling or rejecting thoughts. Rather, every thought, feeling and expression is allowed to arise and pass without the reification and judgement inherent in dualistic positioning.

RELYING ON WORDS

Reliance on words cannot bring us to awakening

Whereas relaxing and releasing all that we have gathered

Immediately reveals non-dual presence.

When we start to move about and talk with others

There are many hooks to pull us into reliance on concepts.

Don't try to be clear, just relax.

There is no need to make any effort

Simply remain open.

The sun ceaselessly radiates light without substance.

The pure ground of being offers self-liberating moments without limit.

When we are sitting in meditation and a thought presents itself, we don't have a front door with a bell on it; the thought is already in our mind. We don't have a choice, it's here. Similarly, we do not pause in front of a thought and consider, *"Oh, is this an interesting thought to enter?"* We have already entered the thought and merged in it as if we were the thinker that created it. Seemingly, without any effort we are in whatever is arising, and then we are not. There is no obvious front door or back door. The mind is open and empty; subject forms and object forms co-emerge and then vanish in endless play.

If you have bad times, you may feel bad yet these bad times don't define who you truly are. If you get a bit crazy for a while, if you are treated badly, if you feel collapsed or worthless and life seems to lose its meaning, these are just transient episodes in the flow of your experience. If you can relax and be with what is occurring, you will see that it passes. We are not the content of our mind and yet we are inseparable from the content of our mind. The content of our mind is experience, our experience—yet no experience can give a total or final definition of who we are or what our value is.

We are here, alive—so simply attend to the immediate presence of awareness that is our open ground, the ever-present basis of all our experience. Simply be aware, be present in, with and as the flow of experience. Observe how each movement is a gesture in space and time and is simultaneously an expression or revelation of ungraspable presence. Our open potential shows many forms, as self and other, yet no appearance can define this potential or predict how it will unfold.

Our life is revealed through being with others. Our life comes to us, is given to us, when we make the gesture of welcoming the other. Sometimes we are happy and sometimes we are sad, but either way, the mood is a revelation, a transient showing. Experience is not a thing you can hang onto. This is really the heart of the dzogchen teachings. There are no things, there are only moments of ungraspable experience arising within the open field of unborn awareness. The more we see that we are always already integrated in open spaciousness the more each moment is fine just as it is.

To open and see what is here is the purest form of phenomenology. It is allowing the world to be as it is and allowing ourselves to be as we are. You could say that this is the basis of a profound non-violence. Although the desire to develop ourselves and increase our good qualities seems to be a beautiful intention, it is actually a limiting obscuration. For every time we have an idea of who we should be and we try to become that idea, what we are actually doing is engaging in violence against how we are now. We are saying, *"I am not good enough. I should be different from this. I would be better off if I were somebody else."* Thus, our hope of betterment starts with an act of self-attack, of trying to transform ourselves without even truly seeing the actuality of the one we want to transform. The hostility of this attitude reinforces our dualistic structure: *"I am taking up a position against myself in order to recreate myself in a way that will get more approval from other people and myself."* We will always find new ideas about who we should be. Therefore, the key thing is to relax and open and be present with oneself as one is.

Observing ourselves is always more difficult than we imagine it will be. This is because we cheat ourselves, for we don't really want to know ourselves as we are. We often want ourselves to be nicer than we are; we have an image of ourselves which we try to protect. Learning to observe ourself clearly is not going to be easy if we hate ourself or idealise ourself. Self-image generated by judgement gives us something to maintain whether it is positive or negative. However our mind has great potential and many different thoughts and feelings arise in it—not just the ones we want or have come to rely on. Let your mind show whatever it will and you may be pleasantly surprised. You are your mind itself, your awareness, and all the thoughts that seem to define you are just passing through.

Our assumptions and our interpretations manifest as if they are the owners of our existence. The servant has become the master and the master has been forgotten. The actual master or the mistress of the house is our buddha essence, our open fresh potential present moment by moment. The servant is thoughts, feelings, sensations. These arisings are sources of information and pathways of manifestation but they shouldn't be sitting on the central throne.

The root of our practice is to be kind to ourself, for through this tender intimacy we find our open availability and so are kind to others. Kindness does not mean letting ourselves off the hook, but it does mean not putting ourselves on the hook in the first place. Being hooked is not very helpful. Judging and criticising is not likely to free us or to reveal our loving kindness.

Tenderness is very important for practice. Outside in the big world there is plenty of violence and we also are often critical and violent towards ourselves. Mistakes, errors and confusions should be recognised honestly and responded to effectively but should not be taken as definitive.

Buddhist teachings say that everything is an illusion. What does this mean? Let's consider this cup I hold in my hand. The experience we have of there being a self-existing cup with all the qualities and possibilities intrinsic to it is an illusion. 'Illusion' means that we forget that subject and object are always born together. The cup-ness of the cup doesn't live in the cup. It exists in our own mind. It is our thoughts that confer individuality and substantial reality to this appearance. Our thoughts make the cup seem real. Our thoughts sustain the delusion that the cup is self-existing. And these thoughts, how strong and reliable are they? Try to catch one and see if it's made of steel.

Whatever comes, comes. This seems to bring us to the crossroads where either I try to improve the object and work hard, or focus on the one who is the one having the experience. Yet dzogchen is the integration of the space of occurrence, the clarity illuminating the occurrence and the ever-changing energy forming as the occurrence. Non-dual presence has no choices to make.

The key point is to be present with whatever is occurring. That's all. Nothing else.

Each moment that we are here together vanishes as soon as it arises. We can make a story which points to the continuity of our time together, yet all the moments of the story vanish even as they are spoken or written. This ungraspable impermanence is not a mistake or a punishment. In fact it is the effortless self-liberation of all phenomena. Everything appears yet nothing remains.

The time for focussed observation of the mind is during the early stages of our meditation practice. Observation lets us see through all that obscures presence. We practise resting in open presence. When we bring our presence into being in the world with others it is time for participation, for being, as we are, a part of the world. We are already in the world. This is our world and if we attend to the world without hesitation or reservation, we will flow as part of its unfolding. We are here, something needs to be done, and we find ourselves doing it. Life is easier when you don't stand outside it and have to rely on concepts to work out what to do.

The less self-referential we are, the more we will find that qualities like generosity and patience are naturally present, and we will want to use these for the benefit of all beings. Cutting the root of ego-fixation allows all good qualities to manifest.

Being a buddhist is just another kind of illusion. You can't really 'be' a buddhist, though you can be a buddha. You can 'do' buddhism. You can do what buddhists do. You can 'do' filling butter lamps, you can 'do' prostrations, you can 'do' wearing robes, you can do many activities done by 'buddhists'. Buddhism is a great factory of activity. However, no matter how good a buddhist you are, that in itself won't make you enlightened. Just as, no matter how wonderful the reflection in the mirror is, the reflection doesn't become the mirror. To enter the openness of the mirror, be the mirror. To enter the buddha mind, be buddha—not a 'buddhist'.

Whatever forms we see lack intrinsic definition: the definitions which we give to anything are extrinsic, contingent and contextual. The seeming 'thingness' of things is given to appearances by our own minds' activity of reification. Our own mind puts the thingness in things, and repressing this fact, treats the consequent 'things' as if they were self-existing. These 'things' are defined from the outside by the thoughts we apply to them. All definitions are projections which disguise the intrinsic emptiness of all phenomena. Lacking inherent self-essence, appearances are actually empty like rainbows in the sky.

Becoming nothing you gain access to everything. Nothing is not a nihilistic wipe-out. Nothing allows your narrow self-preoccupation to dissolve, letting you wake up to the fact of your participation in everything. Not being fixed there is spontaneous ease in the flow of becoming.

Truth of suffering

Don't get lost in fantasies about how you think your life is.
Allow yourself to see your core beliefs.
Start to feel the anxiety at their heart.
A heart of anxiety.

Here dwells the root of all our suffering –
Attachment to an image of stability which cannot be achieved.
Endlessly failing to achieve the impossible,
It is we ourselves who torment ourselves.

The root of attachment is ignorance.
You ignore and then quite forget your own ground, your own being.
In not knowing who you are you become anxious.
In order to defend against the truth that your ego self is an illusion
You attach yourself to various propositions, beliefs and assumptions
As if these foreign bodies could establish yourself.

This is personal because it is happening to you.
It is your story alone—and this is your lonely truth.
Yet the structure is not personal.
This structure, the structure of you being you,
Is the commonplace structure of samsara.

Because of ignorance there is attachment
Because of attachment there is confused behaviour
Because of confused behaviour there is suffering.
Your suffering is not a punishment.
It is not a sign that you personally, deeply, intrinsically are bad.

Place your finger in a candle flame and it will burn
Bringing bright pain.
Attachment is our return again and again to the candle flame
In the hope that this time
There will be pleasure.

Just as we see with sadness
The poor moth trying again and again
To burn itself to death
So the Buddha looks down
And sees human beings again and again
Flying with desperate longing
Towards the flaming delusion that consumes us.

You cannot awaken to your buddha potential through study. It is not generated by sophisticated philosophical ideas. Nor is it about developing a body of experience that you build upon. Rather it is a matter of allowing what is here to reveal itself, and that happens when we become open and available to receive what has always been present. Our own hungry activity endlessly searching for what is missing is itself the force that blocks the door to awakening. Strangely, letting go offers more than effortful construction.

Thoughts go on journeys but the mind never moves. The basic clarity of the mind doesn't move or change or go anywhere. How peaceful, how restful. So much of our effort is unnecessary.

As our attachment to habitual concepts loosens we find there is more space in our lives. Being intrinsically open, awareness stays open to all that occurs, and with this both subject and object are revealed as empty of fixed defining essence.

If we chase happiness on the basis of sorting ourselves out, of becoming better people, of removing all the knots and difficulties which make us narrow-minded and selfish, we are then operating inside a paradigm which says, *"I am a construct that can, with effort, be re-constructed to become the right shape."* Yet who is to know and judge what the 'right shape' is? There is no end to self-improvement since our empty self is the great shape-shifter.

Presence is about living our own non-dual complexity rather than trying to simplify our energy by making ourselves a reliable fixed phenomenon. We open to the infinity of our own presence, the spaciousness of our ground-being. This is wide enough and deep enough to provide hospitality and space for whatever kind of experience may arise. The space of awareness is the space for each moment to be as it is, whereas the space of the ego, being restricted and restrictive, distorts each moment, bending it to its own purposes.

The particular quality of dzogchen practice is that nothing in your life has to change. Dzogchen is not telling you to change your behaviour or your beliefs. Instead we look at our behaviour to see what its purpose is and whether it is actually necessary. We look at our beliefs to see whether they are as reliable as we have taken them to be. Dzogchen is not about believing more, or believing differently. It focuses on moving from 'belief about' to 'direct experience of'.

The biggest mistake we can make in meditation is to confuse the content of the mind with the mind itself.

We can always cheat ourselves by imagining that we are more sorted than we are, which is why the more we practise and gain confidence the more careful we have to be.

When we see paintings of the meditation buddhas, their bodies are depicted as being translucent. You can see right through them. That means 'no secrets'. They're not hiding their mobile phones from their partners, indeed they haven't got any pockets. To be transparent means no hiding place. Life is as it is, naked and unedited. In our lives we get into trouble when we hide things in order to avoid trouble, when we don't want other people to know how it is, as it is.

Perhaps we can trust our aesthetic response to the world, the immediacy of the world revealed through the senses, rather than always making our commentary about what's going on. From the point of view of meditation the commentary obscures rather than reveals what is important.

Our consciousness, our personal history, our tendencies, our associations, all of these are manifesting moments or points of energy of coming into being. But they don't remain. This is what is meant by the buddhist notion of no self. It doesn't mean that we don't exist at all. It means that we are not 'something'. To know ourself in terms of personality and qualities is misleading because how we manifest in the world with others is situationally evoked.

We need the breath of the world to come into us. We need the sounds of the world to come into our ears. Receiving the world into the space of the heart replenishes us infinitely. Then our movement in the world is the movement of non-dual responsiveness.

Put yourself, not the method, first. If you think, *"I'm a stupid person and the dharma is very good,"* then how is a stupid person going to do such a holy dharma? True practice begins with respecting yourself, because whether you like it or not, you are in charge of your life. It's not like driving a car, where the police can stop you and tell you that you are drunk and take away your licence. Until you die you have a licence to mess up your life and there are no dharma police going to arrive and stop you. So if it is up to you, keep your dignity and be present.

Intrinsic clarity, the spontaneous light of the mind, is only revealed to us when we stop running around with our torch trying to illuminate what's going on. *"But if I switch off the torch, won't it get very dark?"* We are afraid of the dark so we feel we had better keep the torch on. But then you only ever see what you are used to seeing, the little circle of light that your own torch provides.

A spinning top, a toy played with by children, will keep going around if you keep spinning it. After a while it slows and gets ready to fall over and so you spin it again. If you don't keep spinning it, it will stop spinning. Pulsation between the polarities of duality is the way in which we keep spinning the wheel of samsara. We keep it spinning because we invest energy into phenomena and make them seem real and important. This is what stops the experience of self-liberation. But if you just leave the spinning top of your habit-formation alone, gradually the energy will leave it and it will stop turning. Then, being uninvolved and uncommitted, we have the space to look, listen and awaken to true connectivity.

We can live in bubbles of hope and we can live in bubbles of disappointment. We can be hopeful for many years and then we can be depressed for many years and then we can be indifferent for many years. Each of these states is like a particular room that we inhabit for a while. Sometimes it feels good. Sometimes it doesn't feel so good. Then suddenly we're in another room and all that seemed so real before has vanished like a dream.

The openness of awareness is easily closed down by the particularisation of our judgement. That is to say we organise experiences in terms of 'This is good and I want more of it. This is bad, or unpleasant or dangerous, and I want less of it. I don't want it near me.' Judgement arises due to reification, prejudice and bias. You can't get fresh food from a mouldy pot.

It is very important to appreciate that the nine yanas, or buddhist vehicles or paradigms, are all just different ways of construing the world, of making sense of what occurs. Each offers an ethos which is described in the tradition as a 'view'. Each view has an associated style of meditation, linked to which is a style of activity. The alignment of these aspects leads to a specific result. These four factors are used to organise the practices of all the different levels or yanas. It is important to understand the view of each so that your practice is integrated and harmonious.

When we lose our way, when we are caught in the spiral of attachment with one thing leading to another, it is not that we have gone from clarity to confusion. We don't get lost by going somewhere else. When we are lost we are still within the open spacious dharmadhatu but we are not awake to where we are. We don't need to travel to find awakening. To awaken to where we are we simply have to stop following the thoughts and feelings that lead us astray.

Why do we take refuge? Because we are lost. We are lost yet we still want to be the boss. Most of us have experienced having a boss who is lost. This is difficult because you can't tell the boss that they're lost. Not a wise move in any organisation. So you have to learn to manage the lost-boss. This is the function of meditation. The ego has to be placated, so that it doesn't get in the way of the work. Developing inner conflict by fighting with oneself is unlikely to be helpful. We need to relax and open but our ego is always finding new things to do. Taking refuge, and especially doing long prostrations, gives the ego an important task to focus on and with that there is peace and calm. With the ego occupied there is space for awareness to show itself.

What is the mind itself? The mind and the contents of the mind are not things to be put on different shelves. When you have mind, you have the content of the mind. Whatever thoughts and feelings you have are not a problem. They are not something to be got rid of. They are how the mind shows itself.

Speaking is a gesture of compassion. Speaking is relational. We speak in order to communicate with others and be available to them. But speaking cannot reveal wisdom. Wisdom is revealed in silence, in profound absorption, in profound attention, in profound opening to intrinsic awareness. This gives rise to certain experiences which we may try to convey to other people, but as we do so we realise it is beyond expression. Sometimes it's better to be in silence. Wittgenstein said, *"Concerning the things about which we can't speak, it's better to be silent."* This is very good advice.

Samantabhadra, the founding Buddha or Adibuddha of dzogchen—the first, the primal, the forever-there Buddha—is traditionally dark blue in colour. Dark blue represents the colour of the sky just before dawn, when the darkness is starting to lighten but there is little differentiation. He is the spacious potential for illumination.

When the texts say we should be 'without thought' this doesn't mean having no thoughts at all. It means that thought is not being used as a basis of identity and so is allowed to pass freely. In our ordinary life we rest on a thought, which is resting on another, which in turn is resting on another. Were you to see thoughts as a problem, then the goal of your meditation would be to gain a state where you have no thoughts at all. However if you have no thoughts, then you paralyse yourself, because you are cutting off the energy of awareness. So when we sit in meditation, it's not about trying to turn off thoughts and feelings. It's about allowing thoughts and feelings to be what they are, which is the energy of the mind, self-arising and self-liberating.

W e have options. We can relax into our own being or we can distract ourself. There is samsaric distraction: running around, making money, causing trouble and so on, and there is dharmic distraction: doing lots of holy practices, accumulating a big altar and so on. If you have a big altar you have a lot of bowls to clean every day. If you don't clean the bowls you feel guilty. However if you have to clean the bowls, then you do have something to do, *"Now I'm cleaning the bowls for the buddha!"* *"Hm...?"* but does the buddha like clean bowls? No, we do these things for ourselves. So what do we get from doing these things? We generate a sense of meaning and value and competency, a sense that we 'know what to do'. We know how to do mudras, we know the right tune for each prayer... You see the danger? You can get lost in dharma just as easily as you can get lost in making money. It is simpler and safer to relax into our own unchanging presence.

T here is a difference between 'as is' and 'as if'. Perhaps as a child your parents made little shadows on the wall using their hands and fingers, and told you a story about a deer walking along. The 'as is' is a shadow, the shadow made by light falling on to the hand. The 'as if' is when we recognise, *"Oh! It's a deer! Look, it's got two little horns..."* In fact it's not a deer at all; it's a shadow. This 'as if' is an interpretation which we put on to the basic ingredient of the shadow. The shadow form arises due to the interplay of hand, light and wall. These three factors collaborate to support the illusion of there being a deer. Our mind itself is 'as is', empty, ungraspable yet present. It shows itself through all of the forms of 'as if': memories, thoughts, associations and so on. 'As is' and 'as if' are inseparable like mirror and reflection. They are not the same and yet they cannot be forced apart. Both 'as is' and 'as if' are hidden when we believe the shadow, the reflection, is substantial and real.

We are very, very lucky to have met the practice of not interfering with self-liberation. It is the sweet gift of the lineage. Observe yourself. When negativity arises and you neither push it away nor indulge it, but simply stay present with it, it will vanish without trace. If you merge into it, that merging creates an excess, which is an energetic charge. If you try to exclude it, this leads to a deficit or lack, which, like a vacuum, sucks in more thought. The practice of self-liberation shows the seamless vanishing of all experience. The more you get used to the self-liberation of negative thoughts in yourself, the more you are likely to be ethical. That is a surprising paradox. The more you accept and tolerate the fact that you are awash with all sorts of complicated and difficult thoughts and feelings, and allow them to be there, the more you find that they go free by themselves. Then your being in the world will be less encumbered, you will be less preoccupied with your own concerns and you will have more space to engage with other people as they are.

EASY DOES IT

Easy does it
Is the way
Laughing, dancing
All the day

Stay relaxed
And always play
Even when the
Heart turns grey

Postscript

I claim the Scottish lineage
William McGonagall set in motion.
His words are quite sequential
And set out his own notions.

Writing lines to convey the facts
The words I use are multiple
Finding rhymes is not so easy
And of infelicities I am often culpable.

DEDICATION

If there is any merit in this book, we dedicate it to all sentient beings
and if there is none, may it dissolve in its own empty ground.

ཕན་པར་བསམས་པ་ཙམ་གྱིས་ཀྱང་།
སངས་རྒྱས་མཆོད་ལས་ཁྱད་འཕགས་ན།
སེམས་ཅན་མ་ལུས་ཐམས་ཅད་ཀྱི།
བདེ་དོན་བརྩོན་པ་སྨོས་ཅི་དགོས།།

When merely the thought of helping others
Is more excellent than the worship of all the Buddhas
It is unnecessary even to mention the greatness of striving
For the happiness of all beings without exception.

From the Bodhicharyavatara by Shantideva

9 780956 923943